The Culture of Spending

A publication of the
Center for Self-Governance

The Culture of Spending

Why Congress Lives Beyond Our Means

James L. Payne

ICS Press

San Francisco, California

The Institute for Contemporary Studies is a nonpartisan, non-profit public policy research organization. The analyses, conclusions, and opinions expressed in ICS Press publications are those of the authors and not necessarily those of the Institute, or of its officers, directors, or others associated with, or funding, its work.

Inquiries, book orders, and catalog requests should be addressed to ICS Press, 243 Kearny Street, San Francisco, CA 94108. (415) 981-5353. Fax (415) 986-4878. To order call toll free in the contiguous United States: **(800) 326-0263**. Distributed to the trade by National Book Network, Lanham, Maryland.

Library of Congress Cataloging-in-Publication Data

Payne, James L.
    The culture of spending : why Congress lives beyond our means / James L. Payne.
        p.   cm.
    Includes bibliographical references and index.
    ISBN 1-55815-134-6
    1. Government spending policy—United States. I. Title.
HJ7537.P39   1991   91-18994
336.3'9'0973dc20   CIP

Contents

III
Controlling Spending

Appendix

Foreword

Congressional spending is out of control. Every year our federal taxes rise, and every year our federal deficit continues to grow. In the past ten years alone, America's federal deficit has risen tenfold. And there doesn't seem to be any end to the spending cycle.

Both the Reagan administration and the Bush administration promised to put an end to unnecessary government spending and lower the deficit by implementing federal budget cuts. But Congress was unable to make these plans work. In the recent deficit-reduction agreement, Congress spent $1.87 for every new dollar of revenues brought in by increased federal taxes, making the nation's deficit even larger. This cycle of promised budget cuts and increased federal spending has made a mockery of America's federal government. The *Wall Street Journal* even wrote a story headlined "Budget 'Savings' Means More Taxes." And critics of Congress are calling for reforms that not only limit the amount of congressional spending, but also limit the length of congressional terms.

So why does our Congress continue to spend so much of the federal budget on programs that are obviously wasteful? According to *The Culture of Spending*, it is because they know no better. James L. Payne argues that the congressman's world is almost completely isolated from what is really important to the American citizen. Every item put before Congress has hundreds of lobbyists who support it and persuade Congress to vote for it, and there is practically no one on the other side saying "Maybe we don't really need this." This isolation has created a congressional culture of spending that makes it nearly impossible for a well-intentioned congressman to do the right thing and not spend money on pointless programs. Instead it has become more important for a congressman to shape the actions of other members of Congress than to represent the American public.

This out-of-control federal spending is of the greatest importance to anyone who believes in self-governance. Self-governance means having control over the decisions that affect our lives. A self-governing society is built upon the principle of responsive government, one that reflects the will of the people. Clearly that does not exist in our current congressional system. *The Culture of Spending* gets to the heart of the problem and tells us how we can stop Congress before it spends again.

Robert B. Hawkins, Jr., President
Institute for Contemporary Studies

Acknowledgments

During the five years that this study has been in progress, many friends and colleagues have given important advice and assistance. For their guidance in the early phases of the study, I am indebted to Aaron Wildavsky of the Survey Research Center of the University of California at Berkeley and to Leroy Graymer of the Institute for Policy and Management Research. Those who made helpful comments on drafts of the work include Robert Bernstein, Morgan Reynolds, David Keating, David Boaz, Anne Miller, James Rotherham, Dorothy Boerner, Phil Boerner, and Chip Mellor.

For their assistance in connection with interviews and background material, I am indebted to staff and members of Congress, including Robert Foster, Thomas van der Voort, Paul Jackson, Don Chamblea, John Sneed, James Rotherham, Richard Stallings, Matt McHugh, Norm Dicks, James McClure, Larry Craig, Ron Wyden, Joe Skeen, and Bob C. Smith, and to many leaders in the spending-limitation cause, including David Keating, Dan Mitchell, Sheila Macdonald, and Larry Hunter.

I am grateful for financial support from the Smith Richardson Foundation, the John M. Olin Foundation, the J. M. Foundation, the Cato Institute, and my parents, William and Elizabeth Payne.

Finally, I would like to thank Robert B. Hawkins, Jr., and Robert W. Davis of the Institute for Contemporary Studies for their role in the publication of this book.

Introduction

WHY IS IT SO DIFFICULT to control government spending? In the United States, there is broad agreement that our high level of federal spending is damaging, yet no one appears able to do anything about it. The problem seems so far beyond human control that legislators have passed a law, the Gramm-Rudman-Hollings deficit-reduction act, to accomplish automatically what they are unable to do as a conscious act of will. As one senator put it, this spending-restraint measure was Congress's way of scrawling in lipstick on the motel room mirror, "Stop me before I spend again."

This book attempts to explain this puzzling addiction and to account for the seemingly relentless pressure for higher federal spending. It focuses on Congress because Congress has been the mainstay of the spending system. The past decade of political experience in the United States underscores the point. In 1981, an administration came into office dedicated to reducing the size of government. After eight years of battling, that goal remained unaccomplished. It can be said that the Reagan administration did not try hard enough, that it compromised many of its objectives and failed to advocate the necessary deep cuts that genuine spending reduction would have required. That charge has merit, and is documented in this book—but it overlooks a larger truth: It was Congress that set the practical, political limits on the spending cuts the Reagan administration dared to seek.

The recent struggles have provoked renewed interest in understanding the causes of the prospending attitude in Congress. Much

1

of the attention has gone to institutional analyses, especially analyses that focus on the democratic electoral process. To win reelection, this argument goes, a congressman must promise voters, or at least voters in special interest groups, the benefits that flow from government spending programs.* Hence, a kind of barter system emerges: Votes are exchanged for government benefits, and government spending increases as a side effect.

My book departs from this traditional and widely accepted perspective. The electoral system, I argue, has very little to do with the spending problem. If all Washington officials were appointed for life terms, never having to face the voters again, the spending problem would remain—or even worsen. This declaration will be hard for many readers to accept, but I shall not ask them to accept it on faith. The longest chapter in this book, Chapter 7, is devoted to presenting theory and evidence against the notion that elections are the main cause of the spending problem.

The alternative theory presented here is that the pressures toward greater spending are not primarily institutional, but *personal*. The congressman, after all, is more than a simple vote-maximizing entrepreneur. He is a human being who meets people, and talks with them, *and is persuaded by them*. To a considerable extent, his views on spending issues are shaped by this persuasion.

What makes this communication aspect significant is the fact that on specific spending questions, persuasion runs in only one direction. On spending in general, yes, much is said against it. As I noted, there is a popular consensus that spending is "too high" and the deficit needs to be brought down. On almost every one of the hundreds of specific spending programs, however, persuasion is strikingly one-sided. Decision makers in Washington find those favoring governmental programs everywhere, while opponents of specific programs are largely absent.

Strangely, this bias in the decision-making system has caused little concern. In an ordinary trial where, let us say, a judge decides whether to assess a fine of $100 for littering, we take it as axiomatic that both sides, the prosecution and the defense, should be represented. If, by accident or design, one side were not represented, we would be shocked—and we would urge measures, such as state-

---

*For simplicity, the word *congressman* is used here to refer to members of both the House and the Senate, of either sex.

appointed defense attorneys, to see that both sides had a full and fair hearing.

Why are we concerned about balance in a trial? The answer is that we believe judges and juries are persuaded on the basis of what they hear. If they hear only the prosecution's case, we fear they will be swayed into making an incorrect or unfair judgment.

We seem to overlook the fact that congressmen are also persuaded by what they hear. To be sure, they are likely to have prejudices and ideologies that may resist change through persuasion. It would be overdrawing the case to say they are putty in the hands of lobbyists. Nonetheless, their views will be affected by the information and opinions they are exposed to day after day. If prospending stimuli dominate their perceptual field, are not they, too, in danger of making incorrect or unfair decisions?

Congress is not a neutral institution in which the pros and cons of federal programs are objectively weighed. It is overwhelmed by the advocates of government programs: the administrators whose status, morale, and sense of accomplishment depend on the appropriations they urge; state and local officials who appeal for federal spending with the same motives; lobbyists who press the demands of the beneficiaries of federal programs; spokesmen for business firms that benefit from federal largesse. Speaking on the other side, as critics of federal programs, there is—practically no one! As one Appropriations Committee staffer estimated it, in the congressional persuasion process, the ratio of claimants to opponents of federal programs is "several thousand to one."

Complementing this one-sided pattern of communications are certain underlying ideas and assumptions supportive of government spending programs. Most congressmen have accepted the *presumption of governmental efficacy*, the belief that government can solve any social or economic problem that attracts its notice. Most of them are also wedded to the *philanthropic fallacy*, the idea that public funds are raised without imposing hardship. Presuming that government money is "free," congressmen spend it as though they were philanthropists, merely helping worthy supplicants who seek assistance. These unexamined premises about the role of government in society predispose congressmen to heed the pleas of lobbyists and program administrators.

Taken together, the one-sided persuasion and pro-government assumptions form the "culture of spending," a comprehensive environment of prospending stimuli that envelop every congressman from the day he arrives in Washington. After thoroughly surveying this culture, it becomes not at all difficult to understand why so many congressmen favor the expansion of federal programs. If anything, the puzzle is how a few congressmen manage to stay fiscally conservative, stubbornly resisting the prospending tide.

This book develops and documents the "persuasion hypothesis," the idea that congressmen support government spending programs because they have been persuaded to believe that such programs are helpful. They have been persuaded to this view, I argue, by the one-sided culture of spending that surrounds them. An analysis of this environment is therefore important to a full understanding of the spending problem. By looking at the persuasion process, we can develop new remedies and tactics for restraining government spending.

I

The Culture of Spending

✦ 1 ✦

The Congressman's World

HOW CAN WE EXPLAIN why congressmen vote for spending? For many citizens, moral failings account for this behavior. "How they can shave in the morning I just don't know, unless they use an electric razor so they don't have to look in the mirror," says one irate taxpayer. "It's appalling the way they all spend for each other's bills to stay in their seats."[1]

Although this view may be a fair characterization of some congressional behavior on spending, it is often adopted too hastily. There is, after all, another possibility, a simple theory that makes no sweeping moral judgments. It is the idea that the congressman has been *persuaded* to favor the programs in question.

A critic might find this hard to believe because in his own environment he sees no case being made for federal action. Most of his friends and acquaintances portray government programs in a negative light: Bureaucrats are said to be inefficient, programs are said to be riddled with cheating, and the Internal Revenue Service is everyone's enemy. The critic, assuming that the congressman gets this same picture, can find no explanation for why the congressman supports spending—except dishonorable motives.

The congressman, however, does not see the world as those outside government see it. He does not hang over the back fence and swap yarns about "gov'ment waste" with his neighbor. The congressman lives in a special world, a curiously isolated world that is dominated by the advocates of government action. He is subjected to a broad chorus of persuasion that incessantly urges the virtues of spending programs. Year after year he hears how necessary government programs are. When it comes time to vote, he does not believe that the program at issue is unfair, or foolish, or harmful, for that side of the picture rarely reaches him with any force. In voting for spending, he believes he is being a responsible legislator, and it puzzles him that outsiders think he should be ashamed to look at himself in the mirror.

Congressmen live and act in a "culture of spending." That, to an important degree, is why they favor the growth of government programs. They need not be seen as cynical hypocrites, voting for programs in which they do not believe. We can explain their behavior by saying they are ordinary people subjected to an opinion climate so one-sided that it amounts to indoctrination.

It does not change this conclusion to point out that congressmen *do* hear criticism about the *general* level of spending. One cannot have lived in the 1980s without absorbing, to some degree, the view that federal spending needs to be restrained to protect the general economic health of the country. Congressmen accept this position. They agree that the federal deficit is "bad" and that, somehow, efforts should be made to reduce it.

This general view, however, is typically insufficient to produce spending cuts because it is so thoroughly contradicted by the persuasion on the *specifics* of each program. This is where the culture of spending operates. It convinces congressmen that each individual program is valuable and important. When you add up the cost of all of them, of course, you have a large total, but from the congressional perspective, this figure is simply the "price" one must pay for all the "valuable and important" programs. What shapes most members' attitudes toward spending is not the general theories relating spending to national economic problems, but the seemingly compelling cases for specific spending programs communicated to them on a daily basis.

Let us take a comprehensive look at the process of congressional persuasion and see if we can visualize what would happen to our own attitudes about government programs if we were fully subjected to it.

"Please Help Us"

A good starting point would be agricultural policies. It is widely conceded by those outside government that the massive systems of benefits and subsidies to farmers have been failures by almost every standard. Under programs aimed at preserving the family farm, agricultural surpluses have been piled up, taxpayers and consumers have been drained—and the family farm continues to disappear![2] What leads a congressman to back these expenditures? Were we in his place, we are convinced that *we* would never favor these unfair and counterproductive programs.

Can we be so sure? Let us see what might start happening to our views if we sat where the congressman sits, listening to the witnesses at the hearings on agricultural programs.

In 1985 many farm credit cooperatives fell into financial difficulties, and the question arose whether the federal government should bail them out with some form of subsidy. Hearings were held and witnesses appeared to explain their situation. One of the witnesses, at a House Agriculture Subcommittee hearing, was Charlene Reiser, a rancher from Valentine, Nebraska. "We are ranchers whose newest tractor is twenty years old," she told the committee.

> Our oldest, which we still used until they took it away, was forty-three. Our one and only pickup is going on ten years old, so as you can tell, we weren't extravagant at all. We always tried to save our pennies and didn't buy anything we didn't need. [But] with cattle prices going down five straight years in a row, and noncompetitive interest rates, we've acquired a loss we will never recuperate from.[3]

She recounted how the farm itself had been mortgaged to the local farm credit association—wrongly mortgaged, she believed, and wrongly foreclosed on.

> We have lost half of our land, all of our cattle, and all of our machinery from what we consider unauthorized liquidations. All we want is a release of the liability of the B stock which, by rights, should be ours anyway. That is the least we deserve after all the wrongdoing of the Valentine PCA and the Farm Credit System. We have had to tighten our belts before, couldn't always get the new shoes or the new clothes that you wanted, but I never thought we would see the day when we couldn't pay the electric bill or even be able to buy groceries, especially after doing an honest day's work.
>
> So we need a change all right, a change in the Farm Credit System. So, please help us. Please help us reorganize a system

that will work and get a good farm bill that will bring us in some income so we can pay back our bankers. Thank you, Mr. Chairman.

Is the reader as convinced as before that all agricultural subsidy programs are unjustified? Are you ready to say, without a qualm and without hesitation, that rancher Charlene Reiser and her blind and deaf eighty-year-old father should simply suffer through the tragedy that has enveloped them, that government should not in any way attempt to redress the wrongs they have suffered?

Perhaps an ideologue would be unmoved, but most of us would begin to feel a tug of wanting to help, somehow. By no means have we been converted into supporters of a multi-billion dollar bailout; it's just that the idea doesn't seem quite so indefensible as before. We have moved a bit of the distance toward actually favoring agricultural subsidies. An infinitesimal effect, of course. If we went back to living our ordinary lives, communicating with our friends and neighbors as usual, there would be no discernible impact on our opinions.

If we are members of Congress, however, the hearing goes on, and we listen to the additional witnesses on this subject of a government subsidy to the farm credit cooperatives. What are they saying? In this particular hearing, which occurred on five days in the fall of 1985, eighty-eight witnesses were heard. They included a few other farmers like Charlene Reiser, spokesmen for associations of farmers, spokesmen for farm credit associations, federal officials from the Department of Agriculture and the Farm Credit Administration, some state officials, some members of Congress, and even a bond trader from the securities firm Goldman, Sachs.

When we tabulate the orientation of each of these witnesses, we find that eighty-three were, like Charlene Reiser, making the case for an increased federal role. Four of the witnesses were neutral on the subject, speaking neither for nor against the idea of a federal subsidy. There was one witness, from a public-interest law firm, who spoke against the idea of a bailout and suggested that the policy should be to "simply let the chips fall where they may."[4] In other words, the pro/con ratio of testimony on this spending issue was 83:1.

Translate that into the opinion movement that could result. If we grant that one witness might move an ordinary person a bit of the way toward favoring a subsidy, then it is not implausible to suppose that eighty-three such witnesses would have an effect many times as strong. Hence, anyone who heard the entire hearing would be moved significantly toward favoring government subsidies—and perhaps a bit back by the lone negative witness. Still, if we dropped out of the process right there, one wouldn't expect much change of opinion. The congressman does not drop out, however. Members of this committee attend other hearings on the subject of government spending for agriculture. When we look at those other hearings, we discover the same extreme imbalance between the witnesses who support federal spending and those who speak against it.

What, then, will eventually happen to the typical congressman sitting on that committee, even a congressman who came into Congress skeptical about agricultural subsidies? In not too many years he will have moved all of the distance toward supporting government subsidies for agriculture. That is, he will become a supporter of subsidies.

Of course, this is an illustrative exercise, a preliminary way of indicating the impact of persuasion in shaping congressional views. Many more things are happening than we can convey in this illustration: Some congressmen enter Congress already persuaded in favor of programs, others are particularly resistant to persuasion, and so forth. As we look more closely at the actual opinion-formation process in Congress, we find that this illustration gives a useful picture of the overall pattern.

Rump Hearings

Although congressional committee hearings are by no means the only context in which persuasion takes place, they are one important forum. Congressmen themselves, as well as staff, see committee hearings as an important way to collect authoritative opinion and information.

The striking feature of committee hearings as currently conducted is their systematic departure from the parliamentary ideal. The key requirement for a rational decision-making system, a requirement endorsed by a thousand years of judicial precedent, is the idea of ensuring the full presentation of both sides of a case. On a subject such as the desirability of a particular government program or expenditure, therefore, hearings should exhibit a balance between proponents and opponents of the program. In this way, congressmen could hear both sides of the case and make an impartial decision. If this elementary condition of balance were missing, we would call the meetings *rump hearings*; that is, hearings with the attendance of only one faction deserving representation.

In an effort to see how closely congressional hearings observed the principle of balance, I made a tabulation of the witnesses at a number of congressional committee hearings on federal programs and appropriations. I assembled a broad sample of the different kinds of hearings, ranging from routine sessions before appropriations subcommittees to special hearings on unusual subjects. The overall results, shown in Table 1.1, are unequivocal. Congress does not hold *hearings* on government programs and expenditures; it holds *rump hearings*, proceedings overwhelmingly dominated by the advocates of federal action. Of the witnesses it hears, 95.7 percent speak for the programs and only 0.7 percent oppose them.

This extreme imbalance occurs on every type of hearing, regardless of the subject of the hearing or its announced intent. For example, the term "oversight" does not imply a balanced examination of a federal program; hearings entitled "oversight" are almost always cheering sessions for the program involved. Normally, there is not even one witness present who criticizes the program involved. The *Job Corps Oversight Hearing* (Table 1.1) is typical: All six witnesses spoke in favor of the program. These included spokesmen for the private companies who operated Job Corps centers, the assistant secretary of labor in charge of the program, and a professor of economics who supported job-training programs.

Another of the hearings was entitled *The Job Corps: Do Its Benefits Outweigh the Costs?* Surely, one would think, a hearing with this title would have witnesses arguing for "benefits" and an equal number of witnesses arguing for "costs." In fact there were six witnesses in favor of the program and only one opposed to it. The lone opponent was cast in that role through an accident of politics. He was the administrator of the program who earlier had gone on record with strong endorsements of it. The Reagan administration's Office of Management and Budget had cut the agency's budget, and therefore this administrator was required, by law, to "defend" the cuts—a task he tackled with an obvious lack of enthusiasm. The committee members baited him by quoting his own earlier words of praise for the Job Corps.

TABLE 1.1 Congressional Witnesses' Orientation toward Programs

Subject of hearing (and committee)[a]	Supporters of program or spending	Neutral or mixed	Opponents of program or spending	Total
House				
Agriculture/Food programs (Appropriations, 1987)	253	12	2	267
Housing/Space/Science (Appropriations, 1987)	275	1	0	276
Farm credit (Agriculture, 1985)	83	4	1	88
Appraisal of research (Agriculture, 1978)	10	0	0	10
Job training (Government Operations, 1985)	6	4	1	11
Job training (Education and Labor, 1986)	6	0	0	6
Diplomatic security (Foreign Affairs, 1986)	8	0	0	8
Senate				
Agriculture/Food programs (Appropriations, 1987)	144	3	1	148
Housing/NASA (Appropriations, 1987)	161	2	0	163
Farm credit (Agriculture, 1985)	14	5	1	20
Private-sector feeding efforts (Agriculture, 1983)	8	2	1	11
Job training (Labor and Human Resources, 1986)	21	1	0	22
Volunteers/ACTION programs (Labor and Human Resources, 1986)	8	0	0	8
Foreign aid (Foreign Relations, 1986)	17	5	0	22
Totals	1,014 (95.7%)	39 (3.7%)	7 (0.7%)	1,060 (100%)

a. For full titles of hearing documents and details of this tabulation, see note 7, Chapter 1.

Another hearing had the title *Appraisal of Title XIV (Research) Agriculture Act of 1977*. Again, the title is highly misleading. Ten administrators and university professors came before the committee to urge the need and value of federal funding for agricultural research. Not one witness appeared to suggest that such funding was wasteful, excessive, or unfair. One wonders: If this is what congressmen call an "appraisal," what would their "trials" look like?

Another hearing was entitled *Private Sector Initiatives to Feed America's Poor*. I included it in the sample thinking that surely this hearing would feature numerous witnesses critical of government action. It was not so. Eight of the eleven witnesses were supporters of federal programs. One even called on Congress to "legislate an end to the hunger in these United States."[5] Many of their "private sector" programs were actually governmental ones, with the private organization serving as a conduit for federal funds. Naturally, they were eager to increase the flow of such benefits. Two other witnesses at this hearing described their genuinely private efforts, but made no comment about the desirability of the federal programs. Only one witness criticized the federal "hunger" bureaucracy for being slow, impractical, and expensive, and for the way "it ultimately destroys private sector leadership."[6] Significantly, this lone opponent of government action appeared at the tail end of the session, after all the senators had left and the hearing was being conducted by a staff member.

The "pep rally" character of hearings becomes particularly evident when committees take their hearings outside Washington. Although the ostensible purpose of holding hearings in places other than Washington is to "gather information," the actual intent is generally the opposite. Most of these out-of-town hearings are carefully scripted campaigns in favor of a particular program, and any opponent of the program would be as out of place in them as Buck Rogers in a Shakespearean play. They are held away from Washington to drum up media coverage in the cities where they are held.

Of the House committees surveyed,[7] the Select Committee on Aging has the highest proportion of these extramural "hearings," with one-third of its sessions held outside Washington.[8] They follow a well-established pattern, playing, as it were, the nursing-home circuit. In city after city, older Americans are brought before the committee to tell of their problems and infirmities and, in this way, to generate support for the governmental program sponsored by the committee.

One trend that has accentuated the spending pressure on Congress has been the growth of "sunshine" practices. Starting in the late 1960s, Congress made its committee hearings and many of its committee markup sessions open to the public. The idea was to make the process more "democratic," but in practice, sunshine measures intensified the access of lobbyists. In an interview, the clerk of a Senate appropriations subcommittee described the impact this way:

RESPONDENT: If you wanted to track the growth of the deficit with the opening-up of committee markups to the public, you'd find there's a direct correlation. It's very simple: People are against spending in general, but not against it in particular. So the only people that are interested in the appropriations process, in details of the process, are those who want more money. And they are very sophisticated and clever in going about getting that money. And the more you open up the process, the more people are paid to come up here and—increase spending! There's a whole industry that's grown up whose basic goal is to increase federal spending.

QUESTIONER: You say "grown up" in the sense that you feel you see it getting bigger?

R: The number of lobbyists: You can do a check on this, because I'm sure there's some objective information. But I suspect it's tripled in the last five or ten years.

Inbred Pressure Groups

One index of the flood of lobbyists surrounding Congress is given by the official report on lobbyists who have formally registered with Congress. This listing does not cover all the groups and agents that actually make contact with congressmen, but it is nonetheless staggering. The 1987 list, for example, occupied 49 pages in the *Congressional Record* and contained over 5,400 entries.[9]

In the usual image, a lobby or pressure group is an independent group that brings policy makers a fresh view from outside the government. A closer look at these organizations reveals that this impression is often mistaken. In fundamental ways, these organizations are appendages of government, not independent voices.

First, in a surprising number of cases, their officers are actual or former government employees or officials. A recent survey of 776 Washington interest-group spokesmen and leaders found that 55 percent had held some kind of governmental position (29 percent in the federal executive branch, 17 percent in Congress, and 9 percent in state or local government).[10]

Second, many of these organizations are dependent, to varying degrees, on federal government financing through grants and contracts. The list of groups receiving federal funding reads like a who's who of Washington pressure groups. It includes the AFL-CIO, the International Association of Machinists, the American Bar Association, the National Council of Senior Citizens, the National Organization for Women, the League of Women Voters, Planned Parenthood, the League of United Latin American Citizens, the National Council of Churches, the National Wildlife Federation, the Sierra Club, and literally hundreds of others.[11] Leaders of such federally dependent interest groups should not be seen as representing independent citizen opinion. They are quasi-governmental officials with a vested interest in the spending programs that benefit their organizations.

Although representatives of pressure groups are indeed numerous, they are not the largest group of witnesses persuading congressmen to spend, at least not in committee hearings. As shown in Table 1.2, they are outnumbered by the federal administrators who appear to explain and defend their programs. Another large group of witnesses are the state and local officials who come to Washington to plead for federal programs. Congressmen themselves constitute another significant category of witnesses. In what seems a rather incestuous practice, committees allow congressmen not on the committee

TABLE 1.2 Backgrounds of Congressional Witnesses

Federal administrators	497	(46.9%)
Representatives of private groups (lobbyists)	348	(32.8%)
State and local government officials	111	(10.5%)
Members of Congress	65	(6.1%)
Representatives of business firms and consultants	39	(3.7%)
Total	1,060	(100.0%)

to come and testify before them; in every case, these appearances are made in support of spending. Altogether, public officials constitute about two-thirds of the witnesses: government officials testifying about the virtues of, and need for, government programs.

One observer gives this picture of congressional hearings:

> When the HUD secretary or the director of NASA appear, they bring with them rows and rows of minions prepared to answer questions on any minor point the chairman or members may raise. Seated behind the rows of agency partisans are layers of lawyers, legal aides, and lobbyists of the clients of the agencies, the funds of which agencies are later funneled to the clients through programs, contracts, or research grants. The witnesses testify in favor of full funding for the programs. The Senate's former Appropriations Committee staff director, who served for a quarter of a century, noted that in all those years not one witness in a thousand opposed the funding.[12]

The one-sidedness of the committee-hearing process can be especially unfortunate when Congress attempts to act in response to dramatic problems or emergencies. Down through the years, many of the largest governmental programs have been put in place as a rather hasty response to what is perceived as a "crisis."[13] In attempting to react to such problems, Congress is often left without any significant criticism of the governmental programs being proposed.

In 1986, for example, the Reagan administration proposed a $4.4-billion program to upgrade the security of diplomatic personnel and facilities abroad, a program developed to respond to the "crisis" of terrorism. A subcommittee of the House Foreign Affairs Committee held hearings on the proposal (*The Diplomatic Security Program*, Table 1.1). Eight witnesses testified. Five were administrators from the State Department and related agencies who supported the program. In addition, spokesmen appeared for associations of architects, of contractors, and of consulting engineers, all of whom warmly backed the program, pointing out that their members were eager to perform the contracts for the construction work involved.

No one spoke against the program. No one pointed out the absurdity of a $110-million "pillbox" embassy in Beirut; no one suggested embassy closure as a possible response to terrorism in some countries; no one suggested that the danger had been exaggerated for certain countries; no one pointed out that the expenditures would not be effective against most types of terrorism anyway; no one pointed out that the State Department slipped its foreign construction "wish list" into the measure.

All the congressmen could see was a comprehensive proposal endorsed by the president to deal with a grave "crisis," a proposal unanimously backed by the "expert" witnesses. As far as the typical congressman was concerned, it was an overwhelming case. Not surprisingly, the actual vote in the House was 389 in favor of authorizing the program and only 7 opposed.

Congressmen are swayed by the persuasive forces at work upon them. To be sure, some congressmen do resist, guided by their own ideological compasses or swayed by unusual circumstances. Most congressmen, however, tend to respond to their environment. If 95.7 percent of what they hear is "spend, spend, spend," it should not surprise us to find that when it comes time to vote, that is what they do.

Informal Contacts

Congressmen spend only a small fraction of their time in actual hearings. Most of their contacts with the outside world take place informally, through meetings, phone calls, and letters wherein constituents and other interested individuals make their views known.

Not surprisingly, the ratio of opinion in these informal contacts parallels the imbalance in formal committee hearings. I asked many staffers and congressmen about this issue and they all agreed that those in favor of spending vastly outnumber those opposed. One assistant to a Democratic congressman on the House Appropriations Committee described the pattern this way:

R: We get the majority of the flow of our traffic—talking about the budget—after the president submits his budget in January. Then, after that point in time for about the next four to five months it's just a steady flow of people in here, coming in to talk about what they want in the budget and everything.

Q: How many do you see, on the budget? A couple dozen?

R: Maybe five or six groups of people a day. It probably averages out [to] that.

Q: So you're saying hundreds [of people]?

R: Yes. It's just like a revolving door, and basically everybody—I've been up here for three years, and it kind of overwhelms you when you first get up here, but after three years—their message is the same on the budget. They may have different issues in their issue pack, like health benefits, or insurance, or whatever. But other than that, their message is the same.

Q: So these are really people asking for more spending, or spending in their direction?

R: Yes.

Q: Are there any people who come by asking for just less spending, or saying "cut him" or "cut that"?

R: No. I rarely hear of anybody that says "cut this program or that program." Nobody's willing to do that.

Another aide, who worked for a Republican, was asked if his congressman was ever approached by someone who opposed spending:

R: Me, specifically, as far as getting any visits from people who say, "Okay, when y'all have a markup of the Ag bill, oppose the $15 million for this program." We don't get anybody like that.

Q: Really?

R: We get hit continually with people who say, "You need to support x number of dollars for this program, the other program." We get hit quite a bit.

This same staffer gave a picture of what the mail on the subject of spending looks like:

R: In January and February when the president's budget is presented to Congress and the figures start coming out on what's targeted for cuts or elimination, 95 percent of the mail that we receive is from those people who say, "Protect my program."

Q: These are like . . . ?

R: Like railroad employees, and in the case of Amtrak, it's retirees. It's travel agents, people who have a direct interest in seeing a program like that continued. We see commonly that, in a case like [the possible funding cutoff for] Amtrak, one person will write a letter, make fifty copies, distribute it to all their fellow employees.

Q: It's the same letter?

R: It's the same letter and we get all fifty copies here in Washington.

An aide to a Republican senator on the Budget Committee gave a similar picture of the flow of mail:

R: The senator gets about five hundred letters a month, ranging from interest groups, most of them are in-town interest groups, ranging from that down to petitions, or from constituents, individual letters from people who write on all sorts of things, from Nicaragua to impact aid. They write in about everything you can imagine.

Q: And what's the balance between people who say "cut the budget" and people who say "protect this program," or "expand this program"?

R: Not very many people say cut. I can tell you the people who say cut things are like the U.S. Chamber of Commerce, National Federation of Independent Businesses. Those who are more interested in the economy as a whole and what impact the deficit might have. For some reason H. Ross Perot [the Texas businessman] writes all the time and says, "Keep up the good work. Keep the deficits down." He writes this in about three times a year. But most people write in and say, especially the appropriations letters we get, "Please support this increased level of funding for our program." That's what I would say 80 percent or 90 percent of our letters are for.

This same imbalance occurs when the congressman returns to his district. At the agricultural credit hearing we examined earlier in this chapter, Kansas Congressman Pat Roberts alluded to the pattern of persuasion taking place:

> I just finished up, as did the rest of my colleagues, a 58-county district tour in our big first district. That goes 4,000 miles and takes us about 3 weeks. Every county courthouse stop I made, Mr. Chairman, the No. 1 concern was the stress being felt throughout our entire farm-lending structure.[14]

After being bombarded for three weeks by pleas for help from farmers, would it be surprising if this congressman came to favor a federal bailout of the farm credit system?

This comment suggests, incidentally, an explanation for why farmers are so influential in the American system in spite of their small numbers. Congressmen are inclined to visit their constituency "equally" on the basis of geography, not population; hence, small towns are overrepresented in their district tours. Furthermore, in smaller towns, the congressman's announced "town meeting" will be a social activity especially attractive to isolated rural residents. As a result, farmers are likely to be overrepresented in the congressman's personal contacts and hence in his persuasion "field."

In the case of many programs, opposition to the specific spending is so rare that it would be considered virtually illegitimate. In an interview with one congressman, whose committee supervised National Science Foundation spending, I mentioned that as part of my study I would be testifying later that year against NSF spending. "You *don't* want to fund National Science Foundation?" he asked me in disbelief. When I told him he had heard correctly, he looked at me as though I were a specimen needing preservation in a museum. "I've never heard anybody say they didn't think NSF ought to be funded," he declared.

It is not only the congressmen who are influenced by the pro-spending communications. Their staff are also subject to the same pressures. They read the one-sided mail, and meet the prospending lobbyists, and sit in on the biased hearings. As a result they, too, come to believe in the need for federal programs.

The same thing happens to the staff of the committees. They are contacted by groups and individuals seeking higher appropriations, and the ethos of "open" government requires that these lobbyists be given a hearing. I asked a staff member of one of the House appropriations subcommittees about this practice:

Q: Do the people interested in spending come to see you?

R: Sure.

Q: Are you supposed to see them? Do you see them?

R: Same as I see you. Anybody wants to see me, I'll see them.

Q: And typically, they are seeking funds to be in the budget?

R: People rarely seek to have funds cut out of the budget.

Q: Well, that's my question. What the ratio or balance is between people that want funds reduced and people that want funds protected or increased?

R: The ratio would be several thousand to one.

Congressional staff are an important component of the culture of spending, further reinforcing congressmen in the view that spending is normal and desirable. Of course, most aides have reservations about certain aspects of the budget and feel certain programs could be cut. In general, however, they, like the congressmen, have become persuaded that the programs of the federal government are appropriate responses to national needs.

The Superlobbyists

The foregoing description makes clear that, on issues of spending, Congress departs dramatically from being the objective, balanced decision-making body described in the civics textbooks. On almost every specific spending program, the institution is overwhelmed by prospending persuasion. As a result, congressmen are more than merely persuaded. They do not simply lean toward favoring governmental programs. In many cases, the consequence is much more extreme: conversion! After years and years of being exposed to prospending stimuli, the congressman internalizes such an intense commitment to government action that he becomes its leading advocate. The administrators and lobbyists backing the program become assistants in the campaign for federal funds, following the lead of the superlobbyist, the congressman himself.

It says much about prevailing attitudes in Washington that such zealous partisanship is never questioned. *It is expected that congressmen will become advocates for the programs they supervise.* The ideal of objectivity has been so submerged by the one-sided clamor for spending that congressmen feel no embarrassment in becoming wholehearted spokesmen for the spending advocates.

One sign of this partisanship is the warm personal relationships that congressmen develop with the spending advocates, the administrators, and the lobbyists. In the hearings, the congressmen do not adopt a posture of judicial neutrality. Instead, they side with the spenders, and the spenders flatter them in return. For example, the chairman of the House appropriations subcommittee dealing with the National Science Foundation, Edward P. Boland (D–Mass.) began the 1987 hearings thus:

> The committee will come to order. We are delighted to have with us the National Science Foundation, one of our favorite foundations. It performs a magnificent task, I think, for the nation and has over the years.[15]

Is it conceivable that Congressman Boland could entertain the position that his "favorite foundation" might be a gigantic waste of federal tax dollars and ought to be abolished?

Sometimes a small gift adds to the glow of congressional goodwill toward a program. For Congresswoman Virginia Smith (R–Nebr.), on the House Agriculture Appropriations Subcommittee, it was pecans from the administrators in charge of the government-funded agricultural research:

> Thank you Mr. Chairman. And thank you, Dr. Bentley and Dr. Kinney. We are happy to have you here. We always feel uplifted as we hear all of the good things that you are doing, and I am delighted to have these new products. You know, the last time you came, you brought pecans, and I am so glad you have some more. *(Laughter.)*[16]

The importance of these personal contacts and friendships should not be underrated. Human beings are social animals, and politicians especially so. When all of a congressman's friends and friendly acquaintances are advocates of government spending, that creates an enormous emotional pressure fostering the continuation of even the most questionable programs. When someone remembers to bring you pecans, it's unkind to slash his appropriations.

Another measure of congressional partisanship is the extent to which congressmen appear as witnesses in committee hearings. In the tabulation of the witnesses given in Table 1.2, we noted that congressmen routinely appear before other committees urging the protection or expansion of the government program at issue. In other words, they are behaving exactly as would lobbyists—and taking advantage of their special position to gain access to the committee hearing process.

Not surprisingly, the more senior congressmen, especially the committee and subcommittee chairmen, become the strongest advocates. They have had the longest exposure to the one-sided persuasion in favor of the programs they are supposed to supervise.

Take the case of Jamie Whitten (D–Miss.), chairman of the House Agricultural Appropriations Subcommittee, and also chairman of the full appropriations committee. This seventy-nine-year-old congressman has served for over fifty years, making him the most senior member of Congress. Over the decades, he has been the recipient of tens of thousands of oral and written communications on the subject of spending for agricultural programs, and, from what we know about the balance of such communications, these have run about 96 percent in favor of spending. This congressman has heard, year after year, the puffed-up oratory of administrators and lobbyists about how vital federal support is to the well-being of farmers, to the preservation of the family farm, to the consumers, to the health of the American economy, and so on—and now, finally, he believes it, hook, line, and sinker. Whereas outside observers feel that government programs in agriculture have sown disaster, he believes the Department of Agriculture has saved us:

> But I will say here, that people in this country don't fully appreciate the great job the Department of Agriculture has done to make it possible for 2.5 percent of the people on the farms to produce the food and fibers for the rest of us.[17]

In Jamie Whitten, the culture of spending has produced a militant advocate of federal agricultural spending. In the House of Representatives, he is referred to as the "permanent secretary of agriculture," the congressman who will defend federal programs even more ardently than the administrators in charge of them. Even though he is chairman of the House Appropriations Committee, he does not see himself as balancing the needs of taxpayers against the demands of farmers. Instead, as he himself declares of his appropriations subcommittee, "We represent the American farmer."[18]

As the Reagan administration attempted to trim back the agriculture programs in the 1980s, Whitten used his formidable authority to block budget cuts. In an extreme move in the fall of 1987, he attempted to punish certain Reagan administration officials who had forwarded the administration's proposed cuts. For example, for proposing cuts in the soil conservation subsidies, Whitten's committee abolished the job of Assistant Secretary George S. Dunlop. In its report, the committee explained why Dunlop was being disciplined:

> After several years of continued rejection by the people and the Congress, the department [of Agriculture] continues to submit conservation budget proposals that are simply out of touch with the public interest. Once again, the committee must face the task of restoring funds for the Soil Conservation Service.[19]

Instead of seeking to decide fairly between proponents and opponents of spending, between taxpayers and beneficiaries, Whitten has become a champion of spending. Far from appreciating the presence of opposing witnesses in his "court," this judge finds them in contempt for even suggesting a budget cut.

For another dramatic case of legislative partisanship, consider Senator Jake Garn (R–Utah), chairman of the Senate appropriations subcommittee that handles funding for the National Aeronautics and Space Administration. Garn accepted a trip on a 1985 flight of the space shuttle Discovery. (This was before the Challenger tragedy reminded us of the dangers of space travel.) As a space-flight veteran, he became an even more committed superlobbyist for NASA.

In the culture-of-spending system, the congressmen themselves have become the kingpins. They have been pressured so thoroughly by communications in favor of spending that most of them have joined, and even come to lead, campaigns for more spending. They, in turn, give the system an even greater bias. They organize the rump hearings where only the proponents of spending testify. They attend each other's hearings and testify in favor of government programs. They hound administrators who dare propose spending cuts. They orchestrate the media campaigns on behalf of this or that new expenditure.

It seems a formidable system—until you realize one thing: No one involved in it, not the administrators, nor the lobbyists, nor the congressmen, defends the imbalance it rests upon. The bias has grown up inadvertently, in direct contradiction to fundamental principles of fair play and objective parliamentary inquiry. Therein lies the promise for reform.

✦ 2 ✦

The Presumption
of Governmental Efficacy

IN A BALANCED SYSTEM of decision making, whether any particular government program would be judged a success would be an open question. Proponents would of course do everything in their power to make a strong case for government action. They would bring forth statistics that documented the need for the program; they would argue that nongovernmental remedies were inadequate or impractical; and they would claim that the existing program was fulfilling its assigned task. Naturally, there would be considerable bias in the case that they made. They might use numbers that exaggerated the need for the program, and be quite selective in the evidence they offered about its success.

The bias on the part of the advocates would not be a serious problem, however, because in a balanced system the opponents of programs would see that the case was questioned at each point. They would dispute the exaggerated claims about the need for the program; they would point to the success of nongovernmental alternatives; and they would present evidence about the program's waste, uselessness, and harm. To be sure, these program opponents might exaggerate and distort just as much as the program supporters—and be criticized and exposed by them in turn.

Such an open, two-sided policy debate would enable congressmen to reach sound conclusions about the value of government programs. Of course, congressmen would still disagree among themselves. Their own biases and prejudices would still figure in decisions—but at least they would be exposed to both sides, so that fair judgments would be possible.

As I have pointed out, Congress is not a balanced forum for deciding on the merits of government programs. Citizens may suppose that it is, and civics books may preach that it should be, but the fact is that on most domestic issues, Congress is overwhelmed by the advocates of government action. On the relatively "noncontroversial" appropriations and programs that constitute the bulk of the budget, the typical congressman will hear *nothing* specific against the program as such—while hundreds of constituents, lobbyists, and administrators will continue to reinforce the view that the program is needed and successful.

The constant repetition of this one-sided message does more than persuade the congressman that specific programs should be continued. It shapes his underlying orientation toward government action in general. From morning to night, the congressman hears about how important and how effective government programs are. As a result, he typically acquires a generalized disposition to suppose that *government is the appropriate instrumentality to solve any national problem.*

I call this orientation *the presumption of governmental efficacy.* It is one of the underlying premises of the culture of spending, a bias that shapes the congressman's attitude toward *all* programs. Naturally, it has a powerful effect on spending: If your prejudice is that government is successful in what it attempts to do, you will be inclined to ask the government to do more. In an interview, a high-spending Democrat from the Northwest expressed this position:

> R: [We] ought to have a very compassionate, caring government that involves itself in trying to help solve some of the problems we face in this country. I would vote for funding for education, and for transportation, for constructing public works, health research, for AIDS: things of that nature. I believe the government's there to solve problems. You don't do that by cutting back the funding unnecessarily.

To understand the culture of spending, we need to explore this attitude, to see how congressmen develop the assumption that government is a successful problem-solving institution.

The Heroic Amateur Gardeners of Memphis

"Please provide for the record," asked Congressman Whitten, "a table showing the location of the present programs, the number of participants, the number of volunteers assisting in the program, and the value of the food produced through the program compared to the Extension Service funds expended."[1]

Pouring into Congress every year is a flood of information about how government programs are functioning in the country. It comes from federal agencies, from state and local bodies, from interest groups, from corporations, from universities, consultants, and even private individuals. In sum, this information constitutes the congressman's "data base" for knowing about the policy world, for reaching conclusions about the value of federal programs.

To understand the character of this information, let us look closely at what came of Congressman Whitten's request. It is typical of thousands of such requests he and other congressmen make to administrative departments every year. In this case, the request was made at a 1986 hearing of the House Appropriations Subcommittee for Agriculture and Rural Development, and concerned the "urban gardening" program of the Extension Service of the Department of Agriculture. This was a $3.5-million program aimed at supporting inner-city vegetable gardening, a program that the Reagan administration proposed to end.

The administrator of the Extension Service duly complied with the request, inserting into the hearing record the statistical information requested, a portion of which is reproduced in Table 2.1. The table indicates that the urban gardening program has been a wonderful success. With only a little "seed" money, the Extension Service has catalyzed the production of millions of dollars' worth of crops. The reader conjures up visions of what the program has meant in the lives of needy urban Americans.

Before we get too carried away, however, let us look a little more carefully at the figures. After all, the numbers purport to count things that would be very difficult to measure. How would one decide who are the "participants" in a program of amateur gardening? Is a "participant" anyone who came by the office and asked for something? Anyone who phoned? If the Extension Service "works with" the local garden club, are all of the (alleged) members of that club also "participants" in the federal program? One quickly sees

TABLE 2.1 Statistics on Urban Gardening Program Submitted by U.S. Department of Agriculture, 1985

City	Number of volunteers	Number of participants	Value of vegetables (dollars)	Federal funds expended (dollars)	Not given in USDA table: Production per participant (dollars)	Not given in USDA table: Production per federal dollar
Chicago	126	2,531	275,000	300,000	109	0.92
Los Angeles	83	15,175	2,893,414	250,000	191	11.57
Houston	73	2,793	850,000	150,000	304	5.67
Baltimore	91	6,000	723,630	150,000	121	4.82
Boston	12	9,700	2,250,000	150,000	232	15.00
Jacksonville	80	5,543	1,330,320	150,000	240	8.87
Memphis	97	3,192	1,408,077	150,000	441	9.39
Indianapolis	2	891	1,660	112,500	2	0.01
Seattle	16	300	2,205	100,000	7	0.02
Denver	200	12,000	2,455,389	100,000	205	24.55

SOURCE: *Agriculture, Rural Development, and Related Agencies Appropriations for 1987* (Hearings before a subcommittee of the Committee on Appropriations, House of Representatives, 99th Congress, 2nd Session), part 4, p. 854.

that merely the task of defining and counting "participants" could easily exhaust all the funds devoted to the program.

It would be even more difficult to establish the value of the food produced. One would first have to count the physical production of carrots, tomatoes, and cucumbers in all the little plots around the city. Second, one would have to establish a value for each item. For an economist, the value of something is determined by what it sells for in a free market. Since these vegetables are not being sold, it's anyone's guess what they may be worth. Should the wholesale price apply, or a retail price? What are Johnny's small squashes "worth"? If no one would buy them in a store, the answer should probably be "nothing."

We reach the conclusion, then, that the information requested by Congressman Whitten could not be gathered reliably, at least not at reasonable cost. The figures appearing in the table are therefore almost certainly rough estimates or outright guesses. Now guesses can be accurate if they are objective, but would officials of the Department of Agriculture make guesses that reflected in an unflattering way on themselves and the program for which they are responsible?

Analyses of bureaucratic information gathering indicate that this rarely happens. In one study, the sociologist-author actually worked in the government agency so he could document the different distortions. The employees were required to fill out time sheets so that superiors and legislators could be shown how much "work" was being accomplished in the agency. The writer found that time reports were viewed as a joke by the employees, who put down imaginary numbers: "The records were filled in according to what the official thought would meet supervisory desires. An entire sheet of figures, totals, and balances was thus filled in, times fabricated, and then passed to superiors for inclusion in sectional totals."[2]

Such a process could well underlie these Department of Agriculture figures. The irregularity of the figures is one clue to their flimsiness. For example, the productivity of amateur gardeners should tend to be more or less the same around the country, yet the numbers in the table show enormous variation. The gardeners in Memphis come out over 200 times more productive than the gardeners in Indianapolis. The economic rate of return on the program is also extremely variable—and in some cases unbelievably high. In Denver, each government dollar invested in the program resulted in the production of $24.55 worth of food—a rate of return 2,455 times as high as that achieved in Indianapolis!

The production figures suggest a considerable exaggeration. According to the figures, amateur gardeners in Memphis in 1985 produced an average of $441.13 worth of vegetables. Since garden vegetables produced at the height of the season that year were priced at little more than 10 cents a pound, even in supermarkets, this means that each Memphis amateur averaged around two tons of produce—enough cucumbers to fill three pickup trucks. What we have in this table is not objective information but what most of us would call "propaganda."

Similar distortions characterize the statistics collected to show the severity of national problems. Since these figures are compiled by administrators and pressure groups seeking government intervention, they often exaggerate the wrong to be righted. The massive expansion of the food-stamp program begun in 1969, for example, was fueled by a report produced by the Citizens Crusade Against Poverty entitled *Hunger U.S.A.* Laden with distortions and inaccuracies, the report claimed that "10 million or more" were in need of government food assistance—a figure accepted both by Congress and the news media, even though it was nothing more than a partisan guess.[3]

The magnitude of the errors in these partisan numbers can be seen in recent efforts to estimate the number of homeless individuals. A lobbying group, the Coalition for the Homeless, reported to Congress in 1980 that there were 2.2 million homeless Americans. In 1986 another advocacy group, the Neighborhood Reinvestment Corporation, estimated the number of homeless at 3.0 million. When the Department of Housing and Urban Development tried to produce an estimate in 1983, it came up with a figure of 250,000 to 350,000. Even this number appears to be a great exaggeration, derived as it was from sources with a vested interest in exaggerating the number, such as local welfare officials and shelter operators. Efforts by independent observers to make a direct count suggested that HUD's estimates were many times the actual number. A careful physical count of Chicago's homeless yielded 2,000 to 3,000 compared to the HUD estimate of 12,000 to 25,000. Another study showed that HUD's Los Angeles estimate represented a tenfold exaggeration.[4]

The estimates of the number of homeless made by partisan lobbies, then, may well have exaggerated the problem by a factor of fifty. Nevertheless, these greatly distorted numbers were relayed to congressmen in legislative hearings, and were treated by the news media as authoritative estimates.[5]

The flaw in the process is not the biased numbers themselves. One assumes that in a free, pluralistic society, activists and advocates will always distort the facts to their advantage. The problem is the absence of competing, antispending voices in the decision-making system. Since there are few program opponents to "poke holes" in exaggerated claims, these claims dominate the opinion-formation process. Even if congressmen discount for biases in the material they are given, this does not solve the problem. When you cut a 50-fold exaggeration in half, you are still left believing a 25-fold exaggeration.

The end result of the one-sided distortions is that congressmen tend to be vastly misinformed about the need for, and efficacy of, government programs. For example, Congressman Whitten reported that he was skeptical about the need for a federal children's breakfast program when it was first proposed. A pilot program was instituted and the results, relayed through the system of partisan advocacy, lodged themselves in the congressman's mind thus:

> But surprisingly, the city that had the highest per capita income and least unemployment, when it started serving breakfast the attendance at school increased about 75 percent . . . when the children got breakfast by going to school, they started going to school to a much greater degree.
> So, what I worried about appeared to be wrong. . . .[6]

A moment's reflection tells us that the figure the congressman is repeating is way off the mark, for it implies that nearly half of school-age children in the city were not attending school prior to the adoption of the breakfast program. What is remarkable is not just that the error entered his mind, but that it *stayed there*. There was no thoroughgoing opponent of government action within his circle of staff, committee witnesses, lobbyists, and colleagues to challenge his wildly mistaken assumption.

Eventually, as pointed out in Chapter 1, the members of Congress become part of the system of distortion. They become advocates, leaning heavily on administrators and accepting their pseudostatistics uncritically. We have already noted that Congressman Jamie Whitten is a crusader for government programs connected with agriculture. When he asked for data about the urban gardening program, he was not expecting an objective, balanced tally. What he really was saying was, "Please provide for the record such figures as will tend to support the program in question." And that is what he got.

The Policy Evaluation Industry

In recent years, considerable attention has been given to the subject of program evaluation. The feeling is growing that one ought to be able to measure the usefulness of programs, and in this way decide which to continue and which to terminate. As a result, a large number of policy-evaluation specialists have been drawn into the decision-making process: economists who make cost–benefit calculations, sociologists who study the rates at which beneficiaries of programs engage in desirable or undesirable behavior, and so on. Some idea of the importance of the evaluation industry can be gained from the tabulation of projects for just one agency, the Food and Nutrition Service of the Department of Agriculture, given in Table 2.2. An extrapolation from these figures to the entire federal establishment indicates that policy evaluation has become a billion-dollar industry.

In one respect, this emphasis on policy evaluation is healthy. It implies a concern about whether or not programs are effective, and a willingness to make some type of empirical determination on the subject. In principle, policy evaluation offers a means of defeating wasteful or counterproductive programs.

In practice, however, the evaluation process seldom lives up to its promise. Instead of being a source of objective information, the policy-evaluation system has become an extension of the culture of spending, serving to further reinforce the pressures to spend. The underlying problem is the same as that affecting Congress itself: the lack of opponents of programs. Indeed, it is unlikely that in this entire billion-dollar industry there is even one thoroughgoing opponent of government action. The result is that government programs are being evaluated by believers in government programs.

True critics are excluded from the policy-evaluation process because, simply, they contradict the purposes of those who fund and participate in evaluation projects. There are many different nooks and crannies in the policy-evaluation field but, in the main, this

TABLE 2.2 Studies Commissioned by the Food and Nutrition Service, 1987

Contractor	Number of Contracts	Cost (dollars)
Abt Associates	9	8,720,000
Mathematica Policy Research, Inc.	3	5,000,000
Urban Institute	2	2,500,000
Applied Management Sciences	2	1,460,000
Virginia Tech	1	3,750,000
Quality Planning Corporation	1	900,000
Cosmos Corporation	1	760,000
Professional Management Associates	1	750,000
Development Associates	1	570,000
Analytic Systems, Inc.	1	550,000
Abel, Daft & Earley, Inc.	1	400,000
Electric Strategy Associates	1	300,000
Sigma One	1	270,000
American Management Systems, Inc.	1	128,000
Westat	1	99,000
Federal agencies	4	1,708,000
Subtotal, finalized contracts	31	27,865,000
Contracts in negotiation for 1987[a]	8	7,191,000
Total, 1987 contracts	39	35,056,000

a. This is an estimate based on the average for the 31 contracts where cost was given.
SOURCE: Compiled from U.S. Congress, House of Representatives, 100th Congress, 1st Session, *Rural Development, Agriculture, and Related Agencies Appropriations for 1988* (Hearings before a subcommittee of the Committee on Appropriations), part 5, pp. 306–13.

system is controlled by government agencies that seek evaluations of their own programs. They do the bulk of the evaluation, both with their own personnel and by commissioning consultants or university scholars to do evaluations for them.

That this arrangement is considered acceptable is eloquent testimony to the strength of the culture of spending in Washington. The flaw in such a system of self-evaluation is obvious: It produces biased evaluations of government action. After all, personnel in government agencies will tend to believe that what their agency does is useful. They are not scientists, but activists who want evaluations to demonstrate the importance of their activities. An official who believed his program was useless or harmful would probably weed himself out of the agency even before the system expelled him. Hence, one seldom finds public critics of government action in a bureaucracy.

Privately, some officials may have doubts about programs, but they refrain from expressing them since that would endanger their careers and their agencies. This point emerged clearly from a study I made of the Economic Research Service in the Department of Agriculture. I was trying to understand how the hundreds of economics Ph.D.s on the staff of this agency avoided making any significant criticism of Department of Agriculture programs in their many reports and evaluations. Did they actually approve of all these programs?

In interviews, I learned this was not the case. Some had critical things to say, but they realized that political survival required that they keep these points to themselves. One senior official put it this way:

> R: [You] choose your words carefully, because you want to be around to fight again. There's no need to talk about our rights. We don't have any rights. If I was Secretary of Agriculture and I didn't like what you were doing, I'd just eliminate you.

A researcher described the same mentality:

> R: You have to remember that if you're going to work here, you have to play the game.

The result of this orientation is evaluations and studies that never clearly criticize a program—even when the authors of the studies believe the program is unsound. A senior official in charge of a major review of the ethanol program, for example, privately believed that the program "doesn't make economic sense." "My God," he told me in a private interview, "there's no way ethanol would pay. We've got to have $60 [a barrel] petroleum and free corn before this stuff will pay." None of this forthright criticism found its way into the actual published report—a dull and confusing survey that, if anything, seems to approve of ethanol policy. The conclusion of the report begins with this declaration: "Ethanol contributes to broad national environmental, agricultural, and energy policy goals as they have been defined by Federal legislation over the past two decades."[8] In this way, the administrator's private, critical view of a program became watered down and reversed by the time it reached Congress.

The picture does not change significantly when outside consultants or university personnel are brought in to do the evaluations. It may seem at first glance that outsiders can be more objective, but this is an illusion. After all, who is hiring the outsiders? It is the agency that does the hiring and it will hire consultants friendly to its views. Typically, the consultants are closely tied to the agency—often they are former employees or prospective employees—and they share the same world view as agency personnel. Furthermore, consultants are financially motivated to produce reports that please the agencies so that they will be hired to do more evaluations in the future.[9] As a researcher for one of the larger consulting firms told me, "You don't want to antagonize the agency that's funding you."

One consequence of the bias in the policy-evaluation industry is that much of the research is unscientific. Since evaluators don't face serious criticism of their "findings," they often engage in questionable practices to make the case for the program in question. The field of job-training evaluation, for example, has been notorious for the "raggle-taggle quality of the research in many of the demonstration projects."[10] A study committee of the National Research Council made a thorough review of over 400 job-training effectiveness studies and found that only 28, or less than 7 percent, met "minimal standards of evidence."[11] The committee concluded that "despite the magnitude of the resources ostensibly devoted to the objectives of research and demonstration [$600 million], there is little reliable information on the effectiveness of the programs in solving youth employment problems."[12]

This is not to say that all program evaluators are propagandists touting the virtues of programs regardless of the facts. Many are thoughtful, careful researchers, sincerely attempting to make honest reports. They are sometimes acutely aware of program failures. Regardless of how qualified or sincere they might be, however, agency-commissioned evaluators tend to have one failing in common: They cannot seriously entertain the idea of *no program*. They can find that a government nutrition program has shortcomings, but they would not reach the conclusion that government should not be in the food-distribution business at all. They can be critical of a particular job-training program, but they will not say that government job training is an inherently flawed idea.

In a sense, program evaluators are like automobile mechanics. They point to worn parts and weaknesses, and make recommendations about fixing them—but they assume all along that a car is a good thing and that it can be fixed. It would never occur to them to argue that the automobile is an unsound or antisocial means of transportation. The program evaluators' commitment to the idea of government action runs so deep that they are incapable of truly evaluating the programs they study.

One indication of this bias is the way in which cost–benefit analyses are routinely distorted by evaluators. In principle, this technique enables one to decide whether a government program is worthwhile by comparing its costs to its benefits. Unfortunately, the analysts almost always leave out the two largest costs of government action, the burden placed on society by the coercive collection of funds (taxation) and the opportunity cost of the funds, namely, the benefits that would accrue from privately spending the same money (see the Appendix,"Fallacies of Cost–Benefit Analysis"). Were these two costs included, many cost–benefit analyses that have justified government programs would have their conclusions reversed; they would show that the costs of government action outweigh the benefits.

The main message congressmen hear from the policy-evaluation industry, therefore, is that government programs are successful. A good illustration of this process of distortion concerns the evaluation of government job-training programs. To many outside analysts, these programs have been of questionable value, possibly even inculcating bad work habits and unrealistic expectations about the real world of work.[13] Congressmen are rarely exposed to evidence and argument along these lines, however. Instead, they turn to the evaluations commissioned by federal job-training agencies themselves. In 1986 House hearings on the Job Corps, for example, the centerpiece was an evaluation carried out by Mathematica Policy Research, Inc. This study was repeatedly referred to by congressmen and witnesses for its "positive" findings about the program.[14]

In this entire hearing, no mention was made of the fact that the study was conducted by supporters of the program. The evaluation group consisted of four consultants working closely with eleven past and current officials of the Department of Labor.[15] This imbalance was especially serious from a scientific point of view, because the study employed a highly complex multivariate analysis involving somewhat subjective decisions about which variables to include and how to measure them.

Even though biased, the Mathematica report did contain, buried deep in its pages, information that could have been marshaled into a critique of the Job Corps program. For example, the actual increase in employment levels alleged to be the result of training was disappointingly small. The figures show that civilian male "graduates" of the full Job Corps program had a shockingly high unemployment rate of 42.8 percent four years after completing the program.[16] The most dramatic effect that cropped up in the entire analysis was a *negative* one: For young women with children, the long-lasting Job Corps effect was an *unemployment* rate of 76.3 percent, 16.2 percentage points *higher* than in the control group that had no contact with the Job Corps program.[17] In order to make the program look successful, the Mathematica analysts had to exclude opportunity costs and tax-collection costs from their cost–benefit analysis.

Because no one in the policy-evaluation process—in the consulting firm, in the Department of Labor, or in the committee hearing—had an interest in criticizing the Job Corps program, these points were never brought to light. Congressmen could go away from the hearing believing that a scientific study had proved that the Job Corps was an unqualified success.

One congressman, Representative Matthew G. Martinez (D–Calif.), even supposed that the Mathematica study supported his belief that *all* the Job Corps trainees "went on to a job someplace."[18] In fact, the Mathematica study documented the inaccuracy of this belief, for it showed that all types of Job Corps graduate groups had extremely high unemployment rates—in some categories, over 80 percent.[19]

We have, then, another illustration of how biased sources and one-sided congressional fact gathering combined to leave a congressman badly misinformed about a federal policy. Needless to say, the direction of the congressman's misjudgment was toward presuming that a government program was more effective than was actually the case.

Why Not Presume Governmental Inefficacy?

Otto von Bismarck once pointed out that making laws has something in common with making sausage: Both processes are unseemly and flawed. "If you like laws or sausages," he said, "don't look too closely at how they are made."

An examination of the U.S. Congress confirms the truth of this warning. The legislative process has not progressed in orderliness or rationality since Bismarck's day. If anything, it has become more chaotic. Consider the major budget bill for 1988, a $600-billion measure passed by Congress in a midnight rush at the end of the 1987 session. This 2,100-page bill was pieced together in a series of backroom conferences among influential legislators. It was found to contain numerous clauses and special favors that few legislators knew about, clauses that later became national scandals. "This blind voting is a sad commentary," lamented one senator. A representative called it an "outrage" that members were being asked to vote on a bill "which not a single member has read or understands."[20]

Bismarck's observation about the weakness of the legislative process extends to all aspects of government. Government is often far from being an efficient, rational, or purposeful institution. It staggers, and stutters, and makes lots of mistakes. The U.S. federal government certainly has made its share. Public housing, for example, often turns neighborhoods into disaster areas. One project, the giant 57-acre Pruitt-Igoe complex in St. Louis, became such a dangerous and repulsive slum that, in 1972, its federal builders dynamited the whole thing to the ground.[21] Government programs to develop technologies often wind up as costly failures. In the 1970s, the Department of Transportation attempted to develop an ideal urban transit bus. After nine years of shifting designs and contradictory guidelines, the prototype buses were scrapped and the entire $28 million invested in the project was recognized as wasted.[22] Sometimes government programs even come to contradict their original purposes. For example, the food-stamp program was originally intended to improve the diet of the poor; it now subsidizes the purchase of junk food and in this respect encourages unhealthy diets.[23]

Many books have been written on the subject of government policy failures. One study surveyed this literature and came up with seventy-five hypotheses about why government programs fail. The author went on to examine eleven different instances of recent program failure in the federal government, failure in the housing program, in fishery loans, in public works, in programs to grade fruits and vegetables, in regulating pesticides, and so on.[24]

This massive evidence of failure would justify, it seems, a presumption of governmental *inefficacy*. After witnessing so much ineptitude, legislators could develop a bias against government action. They could become pessimistic about the ability of government to do *anything* right.

Strangely, no such orientation develops. Congressmen continue with a blind faith in the efficacy of government action. A government program can fail in full daylight and congressmen can bemoan its failure loudest of all, but this will not lead them to wonder if government is the proper vehicle for addressing the problem. Instead, in the teeth of program failure they assume that another program is needed.

Sometimes this faith in government strains credibility. Let the reader examine three declarations made about the Department of Agriculture and try to imagine who made them, and the policy the speaker was recommending.

> This Department of Agriculture is the one that paid out the assets that belonged to us all, invested in the agriculture commodities, and then paid it back to the farmer to get him to reduce production through the PIK program—reduce production when we were involved around the world in very serious situations. And they paid the cotton farmer a whole lot of money to reduce cotton because they thought they had a surplus. They did not know what they were talking about. They did not have any surplus.

> They have got the American farmer to reduce his production eleven percent so that our competitors could increase theirs eleven percent, and they promptly did so.

> The Department of Agriculture had no idea that when they put an embargo on the export of soybeans some years ago that we would be giving up our acreage forever, and the farmer paid the cost.
> I was here when we gave Spain cotton at 46 cents and they sold it for 96 cents.
> We need somebody who will speak up and tell the Department of Agriculture what the facts of life are. Whether this group does it or not, I do not know. But I do know the Department has been wrong all down the line.[25]

The words seem to be those of a forthright opponent of government action, and the point he seems to be making is that since government regulation of agriculture has resulted in such a counterproductive mess, we should decrease the role of government and turn to market mechanisms. In fact, the speaker was none other than Congressman Jamie Whitten! This is the same Congressman Whitten known as the "permanent secretary of agriculture," the legislator who bears a major responsibility for the size and scope of government agriculture programs today.

What was Congressman Whitten's point? It turns out that he was not speaking against government bureaucracies that attempt to calculate and control agriculture, but in favor of the creation of another one! The debate on the floor of the House of Representatives in which the above words were spoken concerned an item in the 1985 appropriations bill for agriculture. Tucked away in that measure was an appropriation for $450,000 to fund an agricultural-policy institute at the University of Missouri.

One representative questioned the need for such an institute in view of the fact that the country already has a plethora of agencies, boards, and bodies dealing with agricultural information and policy. To start with, the Department of Agriculture has three separate bureaucracies, costing over $110 million, for this purpose—the Economic Research Service, the National Agricultural Statistics Service, and the World Agricultural Outlook Board—plus a $12-million National Agricultural Library. Then there are departments of agricultural economics in scores of universities and land-grant colleges. Other bodies mentioned as sources of agricultural-policy information were the Kellogg Foundation, the American Enterprise Institute, the Curry Foundation, the National Agricultural Forum, the Congressional Agricultural Forum, the Congressional Research Service, the Congressional Budget Office, farming-industry corporations, and farm and commodity organizations. Since the volume of agricultural-policy information from all these sources vastly exceeds the ability of congressmen to digest it, why was yet another organization necessary? This was the question being asked of Appropriations Committee Chairman Jamie Whitten.

The above quotation was Whitten's defense of the additional appropriation: Because the system of government policy making in agriculture has failed so miserably, he was saying, we need *another government-funded body to correct the situation*. Significantly, he had no basis for confidence in the proposed institute: "Whether this Institute does what it should do or not, I do not know," he told the House. "I do not know how good a job they are doing. . . ."[26]

How deep runs the presumption of governmental efficacy! The congressman is standing amid the ruins of a government policy, and loudly announcing its failure. Yet to address the problem, he calls for another government spending program—even as he admits that his faith in the new program (the $450,000 institute) is merely a blind hope. Congressman Whitten was not alone in embracing this bizarre logic: When it came time to vote, members of the House approved funding for the new institute.

Examples of this kind could be multiplied endlessly. One can hardly take a step around Congress without coming across a failed government program that congressmen are attempting to fix with another government program, without the slightest suspicion that they might be ushering in another failure. Recall that in Chapter 1 we met Charlene Reiser, the Nebraska rancher who denounced the tragic "mismanagement and negligence" of her local production credit association.

The system of farm credit institutions, however, has been largely created by the federal government, and has for decades been under extensive federal supervision and regulation. The federal Farm Credit Administration has as its stated mission "to assure the safety and soundness of Farm Credit System institutions and to protect the interests of borrowers, stockholders, investors and the public."[27] One of the institutions the FCA specifically takes responsibility for is Production Credit Associations, including the Valentine PCA that "ruined" Charlene Reiser.

She was a living example of the failure of government remedies, yet she pleaded for *more* government intervention and regulation of the farm credit system. No congressman pointed out the flaw in her logic—for they too had accepted it: When government programs fail, more government seems to be the only solution.

I saw a small example of this illogic when I visited the Agriculture Subcommittee of the House Appropriations Committee in 1988, in an effort to testify *against* certain appropriations (an experience discussed in Chapter 10). A witness before me had complained that the Federal Crop Insurance Corporation had imposed an impossible burden on private agents by forcing them to switch to a computer system for which the software was excessively complicated and error-laden. To make his point about the burden of government instructions, he placed a foot-thick stack of directives from the FCIC on the witnesses' table. He did not conclude, however, that government programs of crop insurance are inherently flawed because of the bureaucracy and red tape they involve, but urged the committee to improve the system. (The stack of papers was still there when it came my turn to testify, and I was eager to use it to illustrate the principle of government inefficacy; unfortunately I was not allowed time to make any points against spending.)

Another example of this illogic is the federal bailout of the savings and loan industry begun in 1989. The federal policies of subsidy and regulation led to a staggering loss—on the order of $500 billion—that taxpayers must fund.[28] The orientation of Congress was not to withdraw from attempting to manage this industry, but to redouble the program of regulation.

In 1989 a major scandal broke at the Department of Housing and Urban Development. Fraud and influence-peddling led to six hundred Justice Department criminal investigations and the waste of several billion dollars. Many Congressmen seemed surprised, but, in fact, the scandal represented business as usual for HUD. In the mid-1970s over five hundred people were convicted in a similar case.[29] For Congress and its spending programs, the rule seems to be once bitten, twice bitten.

Faith in Government Has Deep Roots

It should be pointed out that the presumption of governmental efficacy is not confined to Congress. The belief in government as a problem-solver is shared, to at least some degree, by most Americans. To give a fuller picture of the difficulty of counteracting this bias, it is worth noting, at least briefly, three of the broad cultural influences behind it.

First, long tradition going back to primitive times defines the state as a divine institution, with rulers being God-ordained agents. This orientation was adopted by Christianity after A.D. 313 when it became a state religion under Constantine. Church leaders preached that rulers were always right and should be obeyed because God was on their side. In exchange, rulers subsidized church officials and carried out persecutions of dissenters on their behalf.

This arrangement continued until fairly recent times and was endorsed even by the early leaders of the Reformation. For example, John Calvin gave an uncompromising defense of this doctrine in his famous *Institutes*. For him, the main function of government was to uphold religion, "to prevent the true religion, which is contained in the law of God, from being with impunity violated and polluted by public blasphemy."[30] Under this doctrine, as Calvin applied it in Geneva, the force of the state was used to punish, even kill, those who deviated from Calvinism.[31] Since in persecuting dissenters the magistrates were doing "God's work," Calvin put them on a very high pedestal: "Wherefore no man can doubt that civil authority is, in the sight of God, not only sacred and lawful, but the most sacred, and by far the most honorable, of all stations in mortal life."[32]

Little by little, this view of government as the agency of God has faded, and now most Christian denominations accept the idea of church–state separation. Even so, a veneration of government remains. Many people see it as an institution with almost mystical powers to heal and save, far more than a collection of imperfect men and women fumbling with problems they may not understand. Look around. John Calvin's definition of government as the "most sacred" calling is still reflected in our practices. Our shrines to government—statehouses, executive mansions—dwarf our churches. Our boulevards and airports bear the names of politicians, not saints. We know that our politicians and bureaucrats are flawed, but we still have faith, as our ministers pray each Sunday, that God will turn the government they operate into something wise, caring, and successful.

Further enhancing our high opinion of the state are the massive resources available to it, resources of both money and physical coercion. It certainly seems at first glance that with all the money in the world, and all the policemen, too, government *should* be able to solve any problem that attracts its notice.

Finally, democratic electoral politics reinforces the presumption of governmental efficacy. To attract attention and appeal to voters, candidates are encouraged to promise what they will do for the country, what problems they will solve. The underlying theme of this idiom of improvement is the assumption that government *can* fix whatever people are worried about, from low farm prices to AIDS, from the decline of school test scores to racial discrimination. When officeholders return to the voters, they are tempted to claim that, through government, they have solved and improved many things. Perhaps, for example, unemployment has gone down. The decline could well be the result of nothing the government did—or even the result of ending some government intervention. Nevertheless, politicians will take credit for it—and thus foster the belief that government programs to lower unemployment can succeed.

The presumption of governmental efficacy, then, has deep roots in our culture and traditions. It is much enhanced, however, by the one-sided character of the policy process in Congress. If the process were balanced, with hundreds of antispending spokesmen swarming around Congress to make the case against government action in each particular instance, this presumption could not survive in unquestioned form as it does today. These critics would try to foster a presumption of governmental *inefficacy*. They would take case after case of program failure and make a general argument: "See, this is what *typically* happens when one attempts governmental remedies."

This is not to say that an antigovernment position is objectively correct. One cannot easily prove either perspective, that of governmental efficacy or inefficacy. They are too broad to be demonstrated in a simple, direct way. My point is that the case for inefficacy needs to be constantly made to counteract the blind faith in government that prevails in Washington. Today, most congressmen are wedded to the credo that, as the congressman quoted earlier said, "Government's there to solve problems." If spending is to be checked, congressmen must also hear the opposite contention: "Government makes problems worse." That would make Congress open-minded about the desirability of government action. Such a balance in perspectives would affect the larger culture as well. The media would have the "other side" of government programs to report. In this way, the general societal disposition to look to government for solutions would itself become subject to reexamination.

✦ 3 ✦

The Philanthropic Fallacy

THE UNDERLYING CAUSE of many misfortunes in public policy is the human tendency to dwell on what is *seen* and to neglect what is *unseen*. Psychologists tell us this bias is overwhelming at the beginning of life. An infant seems unable to conceive of the existence of anything he cannot see. If his mother leaves the room, the child assumes she has disappeared forever—cause enough indeed for a good cry! As we grow up, we gain a certain ability to visualize entities outside our view, but it is an incomplete skill. Summer is always hotter in summer than it is in winter.

In matters of public finance, this tendency to emphasize the immediate makes it difficult for everyone—policy makers and citizens—to weigh the value of spending programs correctly. In front of us, on the stage and commanding our attention, are the spending programs and the good they do (or are aimed at doing). We see programs to feed the hungry, to care for the sick, to foster science, the arts, education, and so forth. Naturally, we find these aims attractive.

What we do not weigh are the sacrifices that must be made to fund these programs. These are out of sight, but they exist just as certainly as do the benefits of the programs. Indeed, these sacrifices are a mathematical certainty, since every dollar spent in a federal program is, literally, a dollar *not spent* by someone else for some other purpose. For whatever "help" a federal program represents, there is a corresponding "hurt," or what economists call the "opportunity cost" of the expenditure.[1]

Opportunity Costs

Congressmen are strikingly insensitive to this aspect of spending, and their ignorance about it explains, in part, their enthusiasm for spending. In ignoring the opportunity cost of spending, however, they are not alone. To a degree, we all have difficulty with this concept, because it requires that we think about the unseen aspect of a budgetary process that is already quite complex and confusing.

Before examining how congressmen see the opportunity-cost issue, therefore, it is important to give a more detailed explanation, to expose clearly just what it is they overlook about the hidden harm of public spending. In the modern era, the nature of this harm has been almost completely obscured. Standing in the way of an accurate understanding are two serious misconceptions about government spending.

First, in recent times, we have changed what we "buy" with public funds. Traditionally, government spending was dedicated to supplying "public goods," those projects and activities that could not easily be purchased by individuals. The chief among these was the maintenance of law and order. Since an individual could not efficiently protect himself against bands of robbers, nor against invading armies, government was called upon to supply police and defense services.

The benefits of public spending on the traditional public goods were so dramatic that little question arose about their justification. In the case of police protection, for just a few dollars paid in taxes, the citizen obtained security for his life, his family, his property, and his business. As Chief Justice Oliver Wendell Holmes, Jr., put it in 1904, "Taxes are what we pay for civilized society." For its traditional functions, the benefits of government spending were considered to be extremely high, and not really comparable to the benefits of private spending.

In recent times, the pattern of public spending has shifted. Nearly three-quarters of federal government funds now go to the purchase of *personal goods and services*, things people can and do buy individually: retirement annuities, medical care, education, food, housing, telephone service, electrical power, entertainment and art, and so on. What this has meant is that the traditional justification for public spending no longer applies. In an era when government is funding the purchase of Twinkies cupcakes, we can no longer say, in a spirit of unquestioning awe, that government is buying "civilization" with our tax monies.

A second impediment to a clear grasp of the opportunity cost of public spending is the fuzzy view of the taxpayer. Reasoning from the word itself, those expected to *pay the taxes* are seen in two-dimensional terms, as merely the source of revenues. To the extent that they avoid paying taxes, they seem to be direct opponents of government aims, denying government the opportunity to fund well-intentioned programs.

This impression arises from considering taxpayers abstractly, as mere sources of government funds. Of course, taxpayers are people —full, three-dimensional human beings. They have needs and wants, and the monies taxed away from them would have been spent to fulfill these needs.

What would taxpayers do with their money if it were not taxed away? Once we raise this question, we begin to realize that taxpayers are not enemies of government programs but are already carrying them out. Government has programs to pay for medical services and retirement; taxpayers try to put aside money for medical bills and retirement. Government has programs to pay for college; taxpayers try to send their children to college. Government tries to feed people; taxpayers try to feed themselves and their families. Government has programs to supply housing; taxpayers try to obtain decent housing for themselves and their families. Government has programs to create jobs, train workers, develop technology, and stimulate exports; taxpaying businesses and investors also support the creation of jobs, the training of workers, the development of technology, and the promotion of exports.

To a considerable degree, *taxpayers are also doing what government is attempting to do in its many domestic programs*. In trying to keep their money from the tax collector, taxpayers are not the enemies of government aims; they are accomplishing most of those same aims with their own personal spending.

One perspective about government action that might accord a special status to government spending is the idea that it is government's job to redistribute wealth. This argument holds that government can accomplish a social good by taking from the rich and giving to the poor. This may or may not be so, but the issue is academic. The modern federal taxing and spending system is not significantly oriented toward income redistribution. In the first place, the tax system is only weakly progressive.[2] Many of the federal taxes are regressive, including the Social Security tax and excise taxes on such things as gasoline, tobacco, alcohol, tires, and telephone services. Other taxes, such as the levy on corporate earnings, are displaced into prices, affecting every consumer. Even the income tax itself is not steeply progressive, and the operation of many exceptions ("loopholes") further weakens this thrust.

On the expenditure side, federal spending does not go mainly to the poor. Most federal programs are not even aimed at the poor as such. The Social Security and Medicare programs, for example, are targeted at the elderly, and it turns out that the elderly are, as a group, wealthier (and whiter) than the younger workers who are paying taxes to provide benefits for them. Federal spending is also directed at providing subsidies for middle-class commuters, middle- and upper-class college students, for wealthy opera-goers, for upper middle-class professors and scientists, and for a multitude of businesses and industries.[3]

Many other programs tend to be justified in terms of helping the poor, but in practice their main benefits go elsewhere. Programs of farm subsidy, for example, are justified with the impoverished, bankrupt small farmer in mind, but the benefits go mainly to wealthy farmers, real estate dealers, and agribusiness corporations.[4] Programs of public works are thought to create jobs for the poor, but since they require the employment of high-priced skilled labor, they usually benefit middle-class workers at the expense of unskilled, poverty-level workers.[5]

Even the programs aimed directly at the poor are quite imperfect in confining benefits to the needy. In some antipoverty programs, such as food stamps, there are millions of non-poor among the beneficiaries, and millions of (taxpaying) working poor among the nonbeneficiaries.[6] In other antipoverty programs, much of the money goes to highly paid administrators and consultants. In the Job Corps, for example, this high-priced overhead runs costs in some programs to nearly $15,000 annually per "pupil."[7]

Some might wish it otherwise, but the main impact of federal domestic spending is not to effect a redistribution of wealth from rich to poor.[8] Lateral transfers are the main pattern—not to mention a certain degree of perverse transfer (from poor to rich).

Some would say that this situation involves no important loss, that the government is simply buying the same things people would be buying for themselves. In Congress, this view is quite popular. As one staff member of the Senate Budget Committee approvingly told me, "It evens out. Everybody pays for everyone else's goods."

Unfortunately, this is culture-of-spending ideology, not sound economics. When the government purchases what people can buy for themselves, two additional costs are introduced: the cost of taxation, including the distortion of incentives governing production; and the cost of administration, including the distortion of incentives governing consumption. Calculating these costs is quite difficult, but preliminary estimates suggest that for each dollar the federal government recycles through the taxation-subsidy system it wastes more than one additional dollar.[9] Clearly, the system in which everyone pays for everyone else's goods through government taxation and spending is extremely wasteful.

"He Continually Fought for Federal Dollars"

By and large, congressmen are unaware of the opportunity-cost issue. To a considerable extent, their ignorance can be traced to the distorting effect of the culture of spending. In a balanced system of considering government programs, with opponents of programs represented alongside proponents, the opportunity-cost issue would be raised again and again. Hundreds of ordinary Americans would come before Congress to describe in detail the worthy and legitimate uses of their income and implore congressmen, on this basis, not to take so much of it away. Congressmen would soon come to see that every spending program entails harm to those Americans forced to pay for it.

Of course, the system for considering government spending is not balanced. The taxpayers, who are giving up their income to pay for government programs, seldom appear. Most congressmen see only the claimants for government funds. These claimants are acutely aware that their case would be weakened, if not wholly destroyed, by mentioning the sacrifices others are being forced to make to fund their programs.

With the true source of federal monies obscured from view, the congressman is encouraged to believe that government money is "free," and that he is acting as a public benefactor in allocating it to various worthwhile causes. The congressman comes to consider himself something of a modern-day Lady Bountiful sowing "needed" federal dollars about the land. We can call this orientation *the philanthropic fallacy.* At its core is *the failure to realize that all public monies are taken from citizens, imposing hardships on them.*

Virtually all congressmen are victims of this fallacy to some degree. Indeed, the orientation is so prevalent that congressmen often praise each other as philanthropists. For example, one congressman eulogized a deceased colleague for, in effect, raiding the Treasury:

> As Denver grew to become a major metropolitan city on the eastern slopes of the Rockies, Byron Rogers was cognizant of the associated Federal presence which would be required. He continually fought for Federal dollars and was responsible for the construction of the Federal Office Building and Courthouse, the Post Office Terminal Annex, the Air Force Accounting and Finance Center, and Chatfield Dam.[10]

Only a congressman oblivious to the opportunity cost of federal money could make such a declaration intending it as a compliment. After all, every penny that went into the office buildings and dam was taken from Americans who needed it for urgent and worthy purposes: purchasing clothing, sending children to college, buying eyeglasses, fixing a leaking roof. Byron Rogers didn't give up his personal wealth to build the courthouse and the rest. Perhaps these structures represented a useful expenditure of funds, but many Americans were made to suffer in the process. How can it be complimentary to the memory of Byron Rogers to say, in effect, "He continually fought to take money away from his fellow citizens to build Chatfield Dam"?

In the halls of Congress, nonetheless, it *is* thought complimentary to praise a member for federal spending because the source of "federal dollars" and the pain of raising them is kept so obscure. Congressman Kenneth J. Gray (D–Ill.), for example, frankly brags about getting "pork-barrel" projects for his district: "I am offended because I have been called the 'Prince of Pork,'" he says. "I would rather be called the 'King of Pork.'"[11]

Another speech of praise—this one delivered in the Senate—illustrates the philanthropic fallacy in a slightly different form. The speaker was endorsing the legislative accomplishments of retiring Republican Senator Hugh Scott. Among his accolades was the following:

Millions of Americans—now and for future generations—will
know better health, greater educational opportunity and a more
secure old age, because Senator Hugh Scott has made their
human needs his personal crusade.[12]

The speaker was not saying that the senator had personally sacri-
ficed to bring any of those benefits to Americans. The senator did not
use his own income to fund anyone's retirement; he did not personally
heal the sick. All he did, as a legislator, was appropriate public funds
toward those ends. Where did those funds come from? They came
from ordinary taxpaying Americans who were, among other things,
trying to purchase "better health care," trying to pay for college to get
"greater educational opportunity," and trying to save up for their retirement and a "more secure old age." How can it be a noble "crusade"
to deprive people of these things and then give them back?

Significantly, the speaker was then–Vice President Nelson
Rockefeller. Coming from a family known for its generosity,
Rockefeller apparently assumed that government was just more
philanthropy—and no one in Congress instructed him otherwise.

"Who Are They?"

In attempting to explain why congressmen are insensitive to opportunity costs, we have to note the effect of egotism. Everyone
wants to have a high opinion of himself, and congressmen perhaps
more than most other people. When the congressman comes to
Washington, he is surrounded by beneficiaries and claimants who
are pleading for his "help." He is strongly invited to accept the role
of philanthropist, strongly encouraged to believe that he has as-
sisted people and left the country better off by funding government
programs.

This high self-opinion would be directly threatened if the donors of funds for government programs were brought into the picture. As soon as one recognizes that in order to help some people
you have to hurt others, much of the glow goes out of being a
congressman. For this reason, congressmen are reluctant to face the
opportunity-cost issue. Instead, they reach for rationalizations and
obfuscations that hide the reality of what they are doing.

One Republican congressman was apparently brought to consider the donors of federal programs for the first time by my interview question:

Q: How do you answer the point that even in the case of worthwhile programs, the money for them is in fact being taken
from other people who had other uses for it?

R: Who are they?

Q: Like, maybe they even wanted to feed their families, you
could say. I mean, as taxpayers.

R: The effective level of removal from that area, there is nothing, if it were threatening the food, the clothing, the shelter
areas, I would say that *any* government expenditure would
be under serious scrutiny. But it doesn't affect that level.

Without realizing it, this congressman has assumed that the
thousands of dollars taken away from each taxpayer are superfluous;
that, in effect, Americans are earning more money than they need.

A high-spending Democrat replied to my question about opportunity costs with a *non sequitur* about tax levels in other countries:

Q: When you say the government's to solve problems, how do
you answer the point that in order to solve these problems,
it has to take funds *away* from people?

R: Well, that's the, we have one of the lowest, when you look at
us compared to other democracies in the world, industrial
democracies, we have one of the lowest tax rates of any
country, of almost any country in the world.

Another high-spending Democrat met the issue with one of the
most popular justifications heard for spending in Washington:
Spending reduces spending! We had been talking about the federal
food program for women with young children (WIC):

Q: I'm wondering how you react to those that say that in order
to do this, you do have to take money from other people, and
that maybe you're depriving them of things they need, like
even education or nutrition? Do you see what I mean?

R: Well, what we're doing is spending general revenue raised
through general income taxes.

Of course, those income taxes in general terms are raised
progressively from people who by and large are much better
off than the women that we're helping and the children that
we're helping.

The best self-interest argument is that if this WIC program is not funded, and if therefore these women and young
children who are poor do not get their nutritional assistance,
the people who are paying one dollar in taxes for that nutritional program will wind up paying three dollars in taxes for
the Medicaid assistance that will be necessary to deal with
the sickness. So it's an investment that turns out to be less
expensive than the maladies that will result if you don't
make that investment.

In claiming that spending causes saving, this congressman is
apparently alluding to a cost–benefit analysis done by pro-agency
consultants, whose typical biases we have discussed in Chapter 2.
Notice that the congressman seeks to obscure the hurt of taxation by
depersonalizing it: Funds aren't taken from specific individuals
who need their money for urgent, legitimate purposes, but float into
the Treasury in the form of a vague, impersonal "general revenue"
available to do-good congressmen.

The reference to progressive taxation is typical. For a high-
spending congressman, income redistribution is a factor in his
thinking, but not a central issue. He vaguely supposes that programs are helping the needy and are funded by the nonneedy, but
he does not inquire too closely into the issue. This congressman, for
example, has no interest in abolishing taxes that bear most heavily
on the poorest members of society, such as social security taxes,
taxes on gasoline, tobacco, alcohol, and so on. Furthermore, inspec-
tion of his voting record shows that he consistently votes for spending programs with middle-class and business beneficiaries,
including farm subsidies, small business loans, and grants to corporations to build such things as luxury hotels and golf courses. For
big spenders in Congress today, income redistribution is just one of
many appealing themes. It is not a deeply held principle, nor a
consistently applied policy.

A moderate Democrat met the opportunity-cost issue with the argument that government has to step in because the private sector cannot handle the problem. We had been talking about the food-stamp program:

Q: What I'm trying to get at is the larger issue: As government tries to do almost every function that is done privately, it's obviously having to take private money to do this. So it's almost replacing each private function with a public one.

R: Well, I find the government moves in when there is no private function to provide that service. In other words, it'd be my choice that we don't have a food-stamp program. Churches and local communities would resolve that. But when you have people who are starving. . . . Government moves in when there is no other solution at hand.

This view embodies the common tendency to define problems only in public terms. It is certainly incorrect to say that, concerning the problem of hunger or starvation, there is "no other solution at hand." All 250 million Americans face the problem of hunger every day, and about 230 million of them "solve" it—by working, by being dependents of wage-earners, by drawing on savings, by borrowing, by selling things of value, and so forth. To say that there is "no private function" to combat the problem of hunger is, therefore, quite off the mark.

The people the congressman had in mind, however, were not *all* people affected by the problem of hunger but only a particular sub-group: hungry people who—in fact, or by hypothesis—have failed to solve the problem of hunger in a private way. These constitute the public "problem," the hungry Americans discussed in the media and for whom government programs are devised.

At first, this perspective seems to make sense: One needs a government program only for those who have failed to solve the problem by other means. The danger in forgetting about private problem solving, as this congressman has, is that you implement programs that undermine the successful efforts of the private problem solvers. You vote for spending programs that take away their funds and make it more difficult for them to feed themselves, house themselves, and so on.

Because of opportunity costs, even the "success" of a program cannot be taken as sufficient justification for spending money on it—a point the Washington community consistently overlooks. The president of a biotechnology company, for example, reported to a congressional committee that under a grant from the National Aeronautics and Space Administration, his company developed a neurochemical analyzer with "a capability here-to-for [*sic*] unachievable by any other method." He went on to urge "that this one story about the successful use of this program will prompt you [congressmen] to more aggressively support this program."[13]

This company's discovery, however important, is by no means a sufficient justification for the program. The federal money it spent was taken in taxes from other promising ventures—perhaps from a biotechnology company that would have made a far more important discovery if its funds had not been taxed away. The "success" of a federal program by no means justifies spending money on it. One has to show that its benefits exceed those that would accrue from the private spending of the same funds. As already noted, this point is universally ignored by the Washington policy-evaluation industry.

Some participants have so forgotten about the harm of raising federal funds that they consider mere beneficiary approval an adequate basis for evaluating a program. We see this approach in the following account given by a staff member of a Democratic congressman:

R: One of the programs that I remember—every year we get contacts from people down there—is the expanded food and nutrition program, the EFNEP program. It teaches people how to best use their food dollar, how to provide them and their family the best nutrition possible. I can count on, every year, about two or three counties, getting maybe 15 or 20 letters from people down there about how good the program is. In fact, I took a copy of one letter from down there and let my boss [the congressman] read it, about how effective the EFNEP program is.

Notice how donors have dropped out of the picture. To fund this program, after all, money had to be taken from other people who had good and important uses for it. (Among other things, they were going to use some of their income to buy books, magazines, and instruction on health and nutrition, to learn how to better use their food dollar.) Of course beneficiaries are going to be pleased with the "free" goods and services coming from government, but their gratitude scarcely defines the program's "effectiveness."

Overcoming Tribal Habits

Before we come down too hard on congressmen for succumbing to the philanthropic fallacy, we should remind ourselves that it is not only congressmen who are affected by it. The fallacy is rooted in our culture. One of its sources is the ancient mentality that sees personal and public roles as fused.

Among primitive tribes, any wealth held by a chief would be personal wealth, regardless of how he came to hold it. For example, if he carried away some booty in war, that wealth would be his—even though it was obtained by the joint effort of all the warriors of the tribe. If this chief gave away some of this wealth, he would be said to be "generous," since he was parting with his personal property. In this primitive context, there is no "public" wealth, monies that the chief was supposed to manage but did not personally own.

Only recently has the concept of an independent public treasury developed. In this modern concept, rulers do not "own" public monies. Their position is fiduciary: They manage the funds of others that have been placed in trust with them. Under this arrangement, the old moral evaluations do not apply. A ruler who gives away public funds cannot be said to be "generous," because they are not *his* funds and he is therefore making no personal sacrifice. His own wealth or standard of living is not affected by the disbursement.

Old habits die hard, however. We may no longer dress like cavemen, but our mental garments have not necessarily evolved as rapidly. It is difficult to overcome the tendency to suppose that public officials are spending their own money when they allocate public funds. We call the big spenders "generous" or "compassionate," and those who oppose spending are labeled "stingy." We still enjoy fairy tales where kings and queens are "good" because they give money to the poor.

Consider King Wenceslas, the "good" king who, in the popular Christmas carol, "looked out on the feast of Stephen" and saw an impoverished peasant. King Wenceslas and his page took some food to the peasant; for his benevolence, the King acquired such an aura of saintliness that his footsteps melted snow! It is eloquent testimony to the strength of our tribal presumptions about public funds that no one ever asks the critical question about King Wenceslas: *Where did he get what he gave away?* Everyone seems content to assume that he gave away his personal property.

If King Wenceslas had been an ordinary person, working as a farmer or woodcutter to earn his money, then giving alms to the peasant was indeed an act of generosity and worthy of praise. But almost by definition, kings do not earn their funds by selling something they produce. What supports a monarch, and his castles, stables, banquets, and page boys is taxes. Kings send their soldiers around to the farms and villages and force the peasants to give up chickens, corn, or cattle. Whatever praise King Wenceslas may deserve for giving food to the peasant is surely counterbalanced by the fact that he took it away from others in the first place.

The philanthropic fallacy is a broadly rooted error. In a country that considers King Wenceslas a saint for giving back some of what he took away, why should not the Illinois "Prince of Pork" be well pleased with himself?

And Elevator Operators, Too

From the standpoint of the congressmen, many spending proposals are not compelling issues. They seem marginal in terms of their apparent benefits, or they have a history of scandal or waste. In a few cases, the "need" to be addressed is manifestly trivial, not a burning national problem. As an example, one spending issue congressmen have confronted is whether to have human operators run the automatic elevators that congressmen use in the Capitol buildings. One can hardly say that this spending is needed to insure a just and humane society.

When these questionable, marginal, or trivial spending programs come up for a vote, however, they are often, even regularly, approved. On the 1986 vote to retain the elevator operators, for example, 59 percent of the House voted for the spending. One cannot explain this kind of spending by arguing that congressmen are convinced of the vital importance of the program. Instead, there is a negative consideration at work: Congressmen don't put much value on federal money. Their underlying attitude is that it doesn't really hurt anybody to spend government funds. Keeping the elevator operators seems convenient, and traditional, so they vote "yea." It never occurs to most congressmen that the $91,450 of federal taxes that would be saved by phasing out the elevator operators represents a sacrifice for anyone, that dozens of families could feed themselves for an entire year with these funds, or send their youngsters to college, and so on. Federal money is there for the taking, a harmless "general revenue" that materializes for congressmen to spend.

The philanthropic fallacy is at the heart of the spending problem. To control spending it will not be enough to show that programs are wasteful or even silly. Congressmen already suspect that about many programs and they *still* vote for them. What the opponents of spending have to do is make the full case for the opportunity cost of federal spending, to dramatize the proposition that the government expenditure causes injury by foreclosing the private purchase of needed goods and services.

This is not a message that congressmen are going to be pleased to hear, certainly not at first. Since it is a logically inescapable truth, however, it must eventually be acknowledged.

✦ 4 ✦

Spending Opponents, Pseudo-Opponents, and the Media

"THE SPIRIT OF ASSOCIATION," said the nineteenth-century French observer Alexis de Tocqueville, "is one of the distinctive characteristics of America." The truth of his remark is well demonstrated in the thousands of prospending organizations that surround the U.S. Congress.

When it comes to groups that oppose government action, groups that might agitate against spending, the much-celebrated American impulse to organize has been strikingly deficient. Indeed, until very recent times, there appear to have been no antispending organizations in existence at all.

To some extent, antispending groups did not appear in earlier times because they seemed unnecessary. Most politicians shared the Jeffersonian position that government spending constituted a "corruption" that needed to be fought against.[1] As a result, legislators themselves constituted the antispending voice in government, so that any further representation of taxpayers was deemed superfluous. Even as late as the 1940s, for example, members of the House Appropriations Committee felt their duty was "constantly and courageously to protect the Federal Treasury against thousands of appeals and imperative demands for unnecessary, unwise, and excessive expenditures."[2]

The small size of government also had a bearing on the absence of antispending groups. Until recently, federal spending—except for surges in military spending associated with war—was not large enough to cause concern. Even as late as 1955, total nondefense federal spending consumed only 6.7 percent of the GNP.

These factors have changed dramatically in recent years. Most legislators became committed spokesmen for government programs and agencies, with the result that taxpayers lost their traditional standing in the decision-making process. Government grew at an alarming rate, with federal nondefense spending climbing to 17.1 percent of the GNP by 1980. These changes prompted the emergence of antispending organizations.

In discussing antispending groups, we are confining our attention to nonmilitary spending. Opposition to military spending has a long and broad tradition in the United States, and the organizations opposed to military spending are quite numerous, a point that is discussed in Chapter 8.

Private Organizations Opposing Spending

Only about a dozen private groups in Washington have a significant antispending orientation. These include, first, organizations whose main focus is opposing spending and who lobby Congress on the subject. In this category, there are three established organizations.

The *National Taxpayers Union* is the "grandaddy" of antispending groups, founded in 1969 by its current chairman, James Dale Davidson. A mass membership organization of approximately 100,000, it publishes a periodical, *Dollars & Sense*, and compiles a useful yearly rating of all congressmen and senators based on their votes on spending measures. It employs two full-time lobbyists active on Capitol Hill, and has a network of state-level contacts.

The *National Tax Limitation Committee* was founded in 1975 by Howard Jarvis in California to lead the campaign for a constitutional amendment limiting taxes. (Proposition 13, the initiative to limit California state property taxes, was passed in 1978.) Now headed by Lewis Uhler, the organization maintains a small Washington office that does some lobbying on national spending issues and coordinates certain state-tax-limitation campaigns. It appears to have declined considerably from its size in earlier years.

In 1982, President Reagan created the President's Private Sector Survey on Cost Control, a group headed by corporate leader J. Peter Grace and funded by private corporate donations. *Citizens Against Government Waste* is the follow-on organization, formed in 1984, to lobby Congress for the implementation of the Grace commission reforms and budget savings. It hopes to become a "grassroots lobby," but apparently relies mainly on corporate donations.

In addition to these three groups, other lobbying organizations take up antispending themes on occasion. Perhaps the most prominent is the *U.S. Chamber of Commerce*, which has been a fairly consistent supporter of spending-limitation proposals in recent years. Another such organization is the *National Federation of Independent Businesses*, an organization of small businesses. Beyond these, there are approximately 100 business and trade associations that occasionally allow their names to be listed as members of this or that ad hoc antispending coalition, but their interest in opposing spending is generally rather superficial.

Another lobbying organization with spending as one focus is the Republican organization *Citizens for America*. This group lobbied Congress and the media on a wide range of Reagan positions, including development of the "space shield" (the Strategic Defense Initiative), aid to Nicaraguan freedom fighters, and the MX missile. In addition to these somewhat prospending positions, it has worked on behalf of the campaign for a balanced budget amendment and in support of proposed cuts in certain domestic programs.

In addition to the self-declared lobbying organizations, a number of "foundations" have an antispending interest. Foundations have tax-exempt status and, by law, are not supposed to lobby on current legislation. In practice, there is not much enforcement of this vague regulation: The line between a lobby and a foundation can be hard to draw. Nevertheless, most of the groups in the foundation category do emphasize educational work and have relatively less contact with Congress.

One such organization is the *Cato Institute*, founded in 1977. It emphasizes the dissemination of free-market ideas through the media as well as in its own publications, and tends to remain out of lobbying and legislative struggles.

More involved with day-to-day Washington lobbying is the large and well-financed *Heritage Foundation*, founded in 1973. It pursues a broad range of conservative issues, especially questions involving foreign policy and defense. In addition, however, it supports spending-limitation measures, and issues reports and articles critical of domestic spending programs.

Citizens for a Sound Economy, founded in 1984, is a foundation with a focus on deregulation and free-market economics, and includes a strong emphasis on opposition to spending. Its main efforts go into providing general educational materials for the media and the public, but on occasion it lobbies on certain spending issues.

The *Competitive Enterprise Institute*, founded in 1984, stresses free-market principles and economic competition. Its main emphasis is on deregulation (airlines, auto-fuel economy), but it also supports antispending campaigns.

Another educational organization with an antispending thrust is the *Tax Foundation*, founded in 1937 (and now a unit of Citizens for a Sound Economy). It is mainly a research organization and serves as an impartial collector and collator of tax and fiscal data. In the process, it generates antispending findings and press releases. The Foundation calculates "Tax Freedom Day," for example, as a way of expressing how long Americans must work each year just to pay their taxes, assuming all the money they earned starting on January 1 went to taxes. (In 1989, Tax Freedom Day was May 4.)

Another type of organization is the "antideficit" group, concerned with spending only as an aspect of the federal deficit—which is their main interest. Since these groups also favor tax increases as part of the solution to the deficit, they have something of a fuzzy identity. For example, the *Committee for a Responsible Federal Budget* includes former Republican officials David Stockman and Roy Ash and former Democratic legislators Robert N. Giaimo and Edmund Muskie.

A survey of antispending forces would not be complete without mentioning that many free-market educational foundations exist outside Washington, and these also voice antispending themes on occasion. They include the Foundation for Economic Education in Irvington, New York, the Reason Foundation in Los Angeles, the Manhattan Institute in New York, the Institute for Contemporary Studies and the Pacific Research Institute in San Francisco, the Independent Institute in Oakland, the Ludwig von Mises Institute in Auburn, Alabama, the Heartland Institute in Chicago, the National Center for Policy Analysis in Dallas, the Political Economy Research Center in Bozeman, Montana, and the *Institute for Humane Studies* in Fairfax, Virginia.

In assessing the effectiveness of the antispending organizations in combating the culture of spending, we must first keep in mind their small number. Even by generous count, they number less than two dozen. Their adversaries, the organizations that lobby *for* spending, are many thousands strong and, of course, are reinforced by tens of thousands of federal and state administrators. The opponents of spending are greatly outnumbered—by a ratio of several hundred to one.

Another factor that limits their contacts with Congress is the natural tendency of these activists to want to avoid hostility. Trying to tell big-spending congressmen that their ideas are wrong can be a tense and unpleasant situation. I experienced this problem when I testified against spending in congressional committees (discussed in Chapter 10). Knowing my antispending message was not welcome, I felt uncomfortable about appearing. Most antispending lobbyists prefer to avoid hostility and therefore make little effort to contact those who disagree with them. As one put it, "We try to stick with our friends."

Finally, the effectiveness of antispending groups is limited by the strategy they have adopted. Antispending organizations do not aim at persuading congressmen that spending is wrong. They aim at legislative victories on highly visible spending issues. This means they are more interested in winning congressional *votes* than congressional *minds*. This emphasis on legislative victory has several undesirable consequences. First, it means that little effort is made to persuade congressmen on a day-to-day basis concerning the thousands of uncelebrated spending programs. Second, the antispending message tends to be muted and compromised in the interest of building a successful legislative coalition. The result is that even if the antispending legislative victory is achieved, the congressmen involved go on believing in spending as much as before.

This emphasis on legislative victories may be a response to fund-raising demands. Donors—individuals, businesses, and foundations—are more enthusiastic when battle lines are clearly drawn and objectives are specific and winnable. Perhaps the most attractive of such legislative goals is a constitutional amendment providing for a balanced budget. This, it can seem from a distance, would be a way of restraining spending once and for all. Lobbying for this measure has become a centerpiece of the antispending movement in Washington, even though, as I will discuss in Chapter 9, both theory and past experience suggest it would be unlikely to succeed in restraining spending.

Whatever the reasons—limited numbers, conflict avoidance, choice of strategy—antispending groups seldom contact congressmen to make arguments against specific spending programs. Of the score of congressmen and aides I interviewed, none could recall a single instance of a visit by an antispending spokesman to argue against a specific program. (Most noted that they had received form letters from antispending organizations, but they viewed these written communications as inconsequential.) This comment, by a clerk of a Senate appropriations subcommittee, is typical:

Q: What about these groups that are against spending in general? Do they touch bases with you?

R: No. They don't. . . . The Heritage Foundation, at the beginning of this decade, did a lot of work on how you could cut this, that, or the other programs. But I don't see them physically here. They never testify before our subcommittee. We never have any groups before our subcommittee for cutting programs.

In conclusion, although there are antispending organizations in Washington, these groups do not make a significant effort to persuade congressmen that specific programs are unsound.

Governmental Antispending Bodies

Within the structure of the federal government are several agencies that, to a degree, could serve as a source of antispending information and persuasion.

Office of Management and Budget. Established by the Budget and Accounting Act of 1921, the OMB is the president's agency for compiling a single budget from all the agency and departmental requests. Traditionally, the OMB has functioned as a budget cutter, reducing agency requests before putting them in the final budget submitted to Congress.[3] The OMB's orientation does tend toward fiscal conservatism. As one deputy associate director explained to me: "We have this pervasive idea that there's no one out there to really protect the taxpayer but us. That mindset does pervade throughout the examining corps of the institution." A former OMB staffer described the viewpoint more bluntly: "The budgeteer's view of the world is that everybody's sucking at the federal tit."

In addition to its conservative slant, the OMB can compile extensive information about the weaknesses in government programs. It has a staff of some 300 budget examiners who specialize in different areas of the budget. It is their responsibility to assess program effectiveness, using a broad range of sources and techniques.

Despite its assets, however, the OMB is somewhat limited in its ability to counter the culture of spending. In the first place, in keeping with its ethic of "neutral competence," OMB officials do not feel it is proper for them to argue against programs, either in public or in congressional hearings. The OMB makes cuts in various programs, but these go to Congress unexplained and undefended. As a result, to congressmen, these cuts often appear to be the mindless or heartless action of "faceless bureaucrats."

Part of the reason why the OMB feels it should remain aloof from antispending persuasion is the theory that the agencies themselves should do the job of explaining cuts. As one OMB official put it, "We rely on the departments to go out and sell the president's budget. That's their job and it's their mission." The flaw in this logic, of course, is that agency officials make poor defenders of budget cuts—as noted below.

Another weakness in the OMB is its exposure to culture-of-spending lobbying. Following the ethic of "open government," OMB officials feel bound to meet with and listen to interest-group spokesmen who make the case for higher spending. As more and more prospending groups realize they can lobby OMB officials just as they persuade congressmen, the OMB may gradually become just a further extension of the culture of spending.

Finally, the OMB is a federal government agency. It is inhibited in its ability to make profound criticisms of government programs by the rest of the government structure, by the departments, by the president, and by Congress. OMB officials are technicians who accept most programs as given, to be nibbled at, perhaps, but not forthrightly condemned.

General Accounting Office. The GAO was also established by the 1921 Budget and Accounting Act, empowered to "make recommendations looking to greater economy or efficiency in public expenditures." In recent years, the GAO has stressed this role, producing about 1,000 evaluations yearly.[4] Its studies bring to light fraud rates in medicare, bankruptcies in federal housing projects, and abuses in the food-stamp program. In this way, it does serve to supply some negative information about federal programs.

The GAO's effect is limited, however. First, the body strives for an image of impartiality and high respectability. It therefore shies away from making any kind of general or comprehensive critique of programs. It wants to stay on the good side of Congress, which funds it, and Congress does not want to hear really fundamental objections to government programs. As a result, the GAO criticizes around the edges of federal programs, always accepting the underlying, often fallacious, premises.

Another weakness can be traced to the fact that the organization is an *accounting* agency. It specializes in adding up addable things. Since the major issues in policy analysis involve less readily measured indirect and dynamic factors, the GAO perspective is often seriously myopic.

For a typical example of the GAO's limitations, consider its 1988 report on how the Department of Agriculture forecasts the budgetary costs of the commodity-support programs. Every year, the Department of Agriculture goes through an elaborate process to determine how much the crop subsidies are going to cost. Eighteen different boards, offices, and subagencies within the department attempt to consider all relevant variables—crop acreages, yields, worldwide production, legislative programs, farmer participation rates, and so on—and through a complex process involving calculations, committee meetings, and negotiations, the department projects how much the entire program is going to cost the taxpayers.

The GAO examined this process and, comparing the budget projections with actual outlays, found that the "forecasts have large errors."[5] Not surprisingly, these errors were on the side of under-estimating how much the programs would cost, so that Congress was typically informed that the subsidies would cost much less than they actually did. For 1986, for example, the Department of Agriculture estimated that the crop subsidies would cost $10.4 billion, but the actual cost was an "overrun" of $25.7 billion.

In its report on fifteen years of these forecasts, the GAO bent over backward to avoid any significant criticism of the Department of Agriculture and its programs. It did not point out that if one simply predicted that next year's budget would be the same as last year's expenditures, one would have done better than the Department of Agriculture had done.[6] In other words, junking the entire cumbersome "forecasting" process would not only save the taxpayers' money, but also would result in *better* forecasts.

Furthermore, the GAO refused to raise broader questions. After all, the Department of Agriculture has been trying to make these projections for decades, and it is still ludicrously far off the mark. What does this say about the ability of government agencies to make reliable forecasts on complex, policy-related subjects? And since the Department is so bad at forecasting the facts of its programs, what does this imply about its competence to manage and "stabilize" the agricultural sector of the American economy?

Oblivious to these more significant issues, the GAO blandly concluded that the "USDA needs to improve the management of its forecasting processes. . . ."[7] Its recommendations were empty platitudes about better "quality control," and improved "coordination" that accepted the Department of Agriculture's role as forecaster and manager of the nation's agriculture.

Inspectors General. Each federal department has an inspector general, an administrative unit that undertakes investigations regarding program effectiveness, as well as fraud and misfeasance. In effect, these bodies can function like mini-GAOs, bringing to light some of the seamy sides of federal programs. For example, the inspector general of the Department of Health and Human Services conducted a study that found that 10.5 percent of hospital admissions under the medicare program were unnecessary.[8]

Like the GAO, however, these units are limited in the scope of their antispending concerns. They are not disposed to question the basic soundness of a spending program—nor would they be permitted to.

Congressional Budget Office. This body was created as part of the complex congressional budgeting system adopted in the 1974 Congressional Budget and Impoundment Control Act. The theory was to produce a balanced budget by insuring that the separate spending proposals remained below the targeted spending total decided upon by Congress at the beginning of the year. The CBO was given the job of keeping track of how everything was adding up, "costing out" new proposals so that their budget-busting potential might be known beforehand. In a limited way, then, the CBO plays an anti-spending role when it tells congressmen that their proposed program will cost more than they thought it would.

The CBO rarely goes beyond this level of analysis to criticize programs themselves. As the creature of Congress, the CBO cannot afford to provoke the hostility of its employer.

The Pseudo-Opponents of Spending

In the logic of budget making as currently practiced, the administrative departments are thought to be the source of impartial and comprehensive information about their own programs. Under this theory of impartiality, congressmen give program administrators weeks and weeks of time in hearings to describe their programs and explain their proposed appropriations. Under this same theory, congressmen trust the statistics and reports produced by administrators showing how successful the programs have been.

This theory of neutral administration also prompts the president and his OMB to give program administrators the full responsibility of explaining and defending the president's budget for the agency. This responsibility includes the duty to defend cuts made in spending programs. That is, the president makes the cut in the agency's budget, but the administrator of that agency is expected to explain to Congress and the public why the cut is justified.

Needless to say, this theory of administrative impartiality comes nowhere near describing the reality of how federal administrators behave. Administrators are committed supporters of their agency and its mission. They are believers in government as a problem-solving institution. When they are sent to Congress to defend a budget cut in their own program, they cannot be expected to switch gears and stand a lifetime of advocacy on its head. After all, the really persuasive case for cutting a program is that it is wasteful, ineffective, harmful, or even corrupt. How can an administrator say this—or even think this—about a program he has been supervising?

What happens in this situation is that the administrator explains the proposed cut by pointing to the "need to reduce the deficit" and then goes ahead and gives a glowing account of the program to be reduced. Naturally, he only increases the congressmen's yen to avoid the cuts.

The following excerpt, taken from a 1987 House appropriations subcommittee hearing, shows the pattern. The speaker was the administrator of the Office of Transportation (OT), a small agency in the Department of Agriculture that aims to help farmers transport produce:

> Mr. Chairman, for the past six years I have served as Administrator of the Office of Transportation. During that time, our office has provided significant contributions to American agriculture. . . .
>
> I believe that the people of OT, my colleagues and coworkers, the scientists, the economists and the traffic managers, have helped solved many transportation problems in agriculture. They have developed better shipping techniques, worked hard for those harmed by changing transportation laws and systems, and brought needed attention to the rural infrastructure crisis going on in this country.
>
> For these reasons, it is certainly a most difficult and painful task I have in proposing to reduce the Office of Transportation funding in fiscal year 1988 in anticipation of eliminating the Office of Transportation by the end of fiscal year 1988. While it is indeed a difficult decision, I understand the budget realities facing the country.[9]

The speaker went on to describe the conferences, studies, and directives his agency had produced during the previous year and other "significant contributions" it had made to American agriculture. In the face of this enthusiastic account, it was not surprising that the subcommittee restored funding for the agency—which still exists today.

In the final analysis, only convinced opponents of government action can mount a persuasive case against spending, and these will not be found within government. Asking administrators to defend budget cuts is rather like sending foxes to preach vegetarianism. No one is persuaded.

The Media

On most domestic spending issues that come before Congress, the mass media does not play a neutral role. It represents a major force sustaining the culture of spending. One of the striking features of the contemporary political scene is how journalists can become more energetic advocates of spending than even lobbyists or partisan congressmen. Let us examine two examples.

In 1968, CBS television produced and broadcast a program entitled "Hunger in America." The program dramatized problems of hunger and malnutrition among the poor, and was highly influential in promoting the massive expansion of the federal food-stamp program in the years that followed.

"Hunger in America" opened with one of the most shocking scenes ever presented on television. It showed an extremely undersized baby, filmed in the Robert B. Green Hospital in San Antonio. The narrator said, "Hunger is easy to recognize when it looks like this. This baby is dying of starvation. He was an American. Now he is dead."

Unfortunately, this emotional footage was highly inaccurate. Hunger is *not* easy to recognize in infants, since what looks like malnutrition can be the result of either birth defects or premature birth. The latter was the case for the infant in question. A complete investigation later revealed that it had been born prematurely, the result of an accidental fall by the mother.[10] The case had nothing to do with hunger or malnutrition.

The rest of the show followed this pattern of distortion. It depended on biased witnesses, distorted statistics, and irrational appeals, and almost completely excluded opposition voices.[11] The producer's aim in the "documentary" was not a balanced account in which the pros and cons were argued fairly, but to persuade viewers to his point of view.[12] It was, in other words, no different from propaganda that would have been put out by a prospending food-stamp lobby.

Twenty years later, in 1988, with the food-stamp program grown to nineteen million recipients (twice what anyone had earlier claimed would ever be needed to deal with the "hunger problem"), another "news" story came out on the subject, this time a feature article in the *Washington Post*.[13] A group of congressmen had sponsored an "Emergency Hunger Relief Act." The article quoted at length the author of the bill, who declared that the United States faced a "hunger emergency." It quoted another congressman urging "a new declaration of war on hunger," and a third who decried "the sense of hopelessness of food-aid recipients." It cited a "survey" by the U.S. Conference of Mayors (the group that lobbies for federal aid to cities) showing that the "demand" for food assistance had increased "18 percent" and was going to increase further in the coming year. It vaguely alluded to "growing evidence of the inadequacy of food-stamp benefits," and "other studies" that showed a need for the expansion of the program.

Of the twenty-six paragraphs in the story, twenty-two expressed the case for the expansion of the food program, three were neutral, and only one obliquely questioned the need for it (an Assistant Secretary of Agriculture was quoted as saying that the Reagan administration had already submitted "the highest funding request in history for food assistance programs"—hardly a critique of food programs). The story even contained its "starving baby" whopper: It relayed the preposterous claim that to "keep pace with inflation" the $11-billion food-stamp program "needed an additional $6 billion per year." In his partisan heat, the reporter never stopped to wonder how a 4 percent inflation rate could necessitate a 55 percent yearly increase in the program.[14]

A similar pattern of distortion occurs in television news coverage. Whether the issue is housing for the homeless or AIDS or the problems of farmers, reporting on almost all domestic issues is slanted in favor of higher spending. The need for the program will be emphasized and the arguments against the program will be shortchanged. For example, an analysis of thirty-nine network news stories on the social security cost-of-living benefit issue in 1985 showed that prospending material outnumbered antispending material by almost three items to one.[15]

What accounts for the prospending bias of the media? To a considerable degree, it may be simply a manifestation of a liberal orientation. No less than seven different surveys over the past decade have documented the preponderance of liberals over conservatives in print and electronic news media organizations.[16] The findings of a *Los Angeles Times* survey of newspaper reporters and editors in 1985, are typical: 55 percent described themselves as liberal and only 17 percent as conservative.[17]

There may be more to this prospending bias than the liberal leanings of news personnel, however. First, to a considerable extent journalists are like the congressmen, immersed in a cocoon of prospending stimuli. They travel the Washington circles dominated by the lobbyists for spending programs and by administrators who feed them pro-agency material. We should not be surprised to find that they often become advocates of spending programs.

A second factor at work is the requirement of "good" story-telling. To appeal to a mass audience, stories—including "news" stories—must have certain dramatic qualities. Popularly, we say that they need "good guys" and "bad guys." Communications specialists use a more sophisticated terminology for the same idea. They say that drama must contain "pollution"—some suffering, injustice, or wrong to be righted; and "redemption"—the correction of the "pollution."[18] The stories we like to listen to, both "real" and fictional, incorporate this basic psychological element: David against Goliath, Christopher Columbus against the unknown seas, the A Team against the local dictator. Stories built around these elements keep consumers glued to their sets—and watching commercials and paying cable fees. To make their programs and networks successful, media managers encourage the use of this dramatic formula, in "news" as well as entertainment.

On the news coverage of the typical social problem, this story-telling format creates a bias toward exaggerating the problem and defining it as something that a visible stroke by government can remedy. This, at bottom, is why media coverage of something like "hunger" tends to be exaggerated. After all, if there is no "problem," no fearful, vexing "pollution" to make viewers sit on the edge of their chairs, then there is no "story" in the usual sense. One needs a starving baby, whether it really exists or not.

Government comes into the picture as the protagonist, the only plausible David that scriptwriters can find to go against the Goliath of a nationwide social problem. The truth may be that the real remedy for a social problem involves slow, incremental steps by thousands of individuals acting in their tiny spheres to improve manners, values, and culture. Good nutrition, for example, is the product of a subtle complex of cultural values, motives, and knowledge. One can't make an engrossing story, however, with diffuse "solutions" of this kind. It's like saying that Goliath, instead of being slain by a decisive blow, will gradually lose his taste for fighting as the years go by. There is no drama in these piecemeal, drawn-out perspectives, no easily visible "redemption" for the "pollution."

The use of this formula also explains why news stories on spending are unbalanced, with opponents of the government program largely excluded from coverage. Opponents of spending would undermine the dramatic appeal of the story. They would question the extent of the problem and contradict the advisability of looking to government to try to solve it. In effect, they would say that the "bad guys" aren't really so bad, and that the "good guys" are incompetent, if not somewhat "bad" themselves. This tendency of the media to seek out proponents of government action appears to be one of the reasons why liberal congressmen get much more news coverage than conservatives.[19]

Although journalists are carrying out the distortions, it is the viewing public that is ultimately responsible for them. We want our news to conform to the problem-solving mode; it seems fitting, emotionally satisfying. We want the "pollution" to be simple and scary, some problem worth getting upset about, something we can tell friends about— "that poor starving baby they had on TV the other night."

It is the media-consuming public that accepts government as the plausible protagonist, the hero that can right the wrongs described. Here again we encounter the cultural orientation discussed in Chapter 2, the presumption of governmental efficacy. Americans believe that "government" can fix anything—that it can feed the hungry, house the homeless, advance science, stop drug abuse, and rescue the family farm. Given this presumption, newswriters are virtually required to cast government as the redeemer of social problems. "It plays in Peoria."

Were Americans ever to doubt the efficacy of their government, news coverage would change accordingly. After all, the government could be viewed as a disorganized bureaucracy that often exacerbates the problems it tries to solve. If this perspective prevailed, it would invert the media interpretation of spending programs. Take, for example, the proposed "Emergency Hunger Relief Act" of 1988. Instead of slanting his story to emphasize the need for this new federal spending, the reporter would lean in the opposite direction. The fact that we have a "hunger emergency" after twenty years of massive and multiple federal feeding programs, he would say, proves again the futility of depending on government for solutions to social problems. With this new perspective, the "pollution" would become government programs, and the "redemption" would be getting rid of them.

We get the "news" we want to hear. As long as we assume that government spending programs solve social problems, our journalists will make these programs the heroes of their stories.

II

Testing the Theories

✦ 5 ✦

Testing the Cultural Theory

WE HAVE THUS FAR given attention to a description of the culture of spending, to an examination of who the participants are and what they believe. The culture-of-spending idea is more than a descriptive picture, however. It is also a theory—a theory about why congressmen vote for spending. It says that one reason legislators approve expansions of government activities is that they have been indoctrinated by a highly one-sided campaign of persuasion in favor of these programs.

This theory may seem plausible or even self-evident, as it rests on the axiom that everyone's values tend to be shaped by their environment. Since plausible or seemingly axiomatic theories can sometimes turn out to be wrong, however, it is important not to let the case for it rest on logic alone. We need some hard evidence, too.

Measuring the Disposition to Spend

To test the culture-of-spending idea, we need to show that the longer a congressman serves in Congress and is exposed to pro-spending stimuli, the more in favor of spending he becomes. To demonstrate this, we need a measure of legislators' disposition to vote for spending, compiled from roll-call votes on spending.

One such measure comes from the tabulations of the National Taxpayers Union (NTU). Since 1973, this antispending organization has compiled ratings of senators and representatives based on their votes on spending measures. Especially for the more recent years, this tabulation has been quite comprehensive and sophisticated. For most purposes, it is a valid and useful measure of prospending voting.

For this study, I have developed an independent method of measuring spending designed to yield a theoretically "pure" measure of the disposition of congressmen to vote for spending. The aim of this method is to overcome some possible distortions in ratings such as that done by the NTU. One of the main features of my method is that it separates military and nonmilitary spending. The NTU spending scores combine these two types of spending issues in one measure. This is reasonable if one wishes to *evaluate* congressmen as overall spenders or nonspenders—which is the NTU's objective. From a theoretical point of view, however, combining military spending and other spending destroys important information.

Voting on military spending follows a unique pattern, quite different from what prevails on other types of spending issues. In fact, support for military spending is inversely related to support for all other types of spending. The big spenders on everything in general become little spenders when it comes to military issues, and big spenders on military issues tend to be small spenders on everything else. In Chapter 8, I shall incorporate this surprising pattern into the overall theory of why congressmen vote for spending.

Because military spending is so different, it is best to put the military spending votes in a separate category that can be analyzed separately, leaving all other spending votes to be included in a general (nonmilitary) score, which I call, simply, the "spending score."

This spending score has been compiled for the members of the House of Representatives for the year 1986. It is based on 36 nonmilitary spending votes, votes covering a wide variety of issues, including public housing and antipoverty measures, business subsidies, public works, transportation subsidies, and agriculture. A representative who voted on the prospending side of every one of these votes obtains a score of 36; voting against all of them gives a score of zero. (An absence is considered a vote halfway in favor of spending and is given a score of 0.5.) Full details of how the spending score was compiled are given in the Appendix, "Measuring Congressional Spending."

The criteria for selecting votes for the spending measure were much more restrictive than those applied by the NTU—which based its 1986 House ratings on all of the 219 votes that had any bearing on spending. One of these criteria was the principle that the spending vote must be contested, with at least 20 percent of the representatives voting on the losing side. The NTU score, on the other hand, includes votes that were nearly unanimous. It is best to set these nearly unanimous votes aside since voting on them can reflect factors other than the congressman's orientation toward spending. His vote may reflect a desire to "go along" when the outcome is a foregone conclusion, or a desire to posture for publicity when his vote could not affect the outcome.

Using only contested issues means that my spending score is a *relative* measure. Some congressmen do obtain the minimum score of zero, but this does not mean that they voted against *all* spending. On spending measures that were approved by highly lopsided majorities, they could well have voted for the spending. In spite of this difference, and NTU's inclusion of military spending votes in its score, my 36-vote measure parallels the NTU spending measure very closely.[1] Hence, the findings would come out basically the same if we used the NTU method to measure prospending voting.

This congruence between rather different measures of spending points up the remarkable homogeneity in prospending voting (always keeping in mind the military spending exception just noted). A congressman who is inclined to vote for more spending in one area will vote for spending in another: If he votes for antipoverty spending he will also vote for pro-business spending, foreign aid spending, agricultural subsidies, and so on (see Appendix Table A1). As we shall see in the next chapter, this striking pattern is important evidence bearing on the ideological explanations for spending. Here we need only point out that the consistency in voting on (nonmilitary) spending tends to make one method of measuring spending as good as another. Even if they contain different issues, and different votes weighted differently, the overall ranking of congressmen as higher or lower spenders will tend to come out the same.

The simplest test for a culture-of-spending effect is to show the relationship between prospending voting and seniority. According to the persuasion theory, the longer a congressman has been in Congress and exposed to the prospending environment, the more in favor of spending he should become. In Table 5.1, the data have been arranged to test this idea, and they show a clear seniority effect. In both parties, spending scores go up as longevity in Congress increases. We do notice in the table a very large difference between

TABLE 5.1   The Effect of Congressional Tenure on Representatives'
Spending, 1986

| Number of terms in Congress | Average spending score | |
	Democrats	Republicans
One and two	28.6	8.0
Three and four	29.5	9.6
Five, six, and seven	30.0	11.0
Eight or more	31.3	13.7

NOTE: The spending score is based on thirty-six nonmilitary spending votes. The
maximum score is thirty-six and the minimum is zero. The size of the respective
samples are: Democrats—67, 50, 69, 56, for a total of 242; Republicans—55, 60, 30,
27, for a total of 172.

the parties, with Democrats being much more prospending than
Republicans. A comprehensive account of why congressmen vote
for spending must incorporate this pattern into the analysis—a task
I shall attempt later in this chapter, and in Chapter 6.

A closer look at the impact of seniority can be had by inspecting
the spending scores of the most senior members in the House, those
with at least twelve terms' (twenty-four years') service in 1988. As
shown in Table 5.2, these senior members comprised the most prospending segments of their respective parties. Among the twenty-
five senior Democrats, over half had nearly perfect prospending
scores of 33 or more (36 is the maximum possible), and only two
could be classified as even moderate spenders (with scores of 19.5
and 20). These senior members of the majority party were the officers and leaders of the House of Representatives. They included the
then–Speaker, Jim Wright, the Chairman of the Appropriations
Committee, Jamie Whitten, and the chairmen of most of the other
House committees. These high-spending senior Democrats set the
tone and direct the business of the House. Among the senior Republicans, the effect of long service is dramatic. Three of the seven members in this group had spending scores comparable to Democratic
scores, and two had spending scores in the moderate range. In the
group, only two, Michel and Latta, had clearly low scores.

This relationship between longer tenure in Congress and more
prospending attitudes is not an artifact of the year or issues chosen.
Using a spending scale based on different votes in the 1984 session,
I found the same relationship between seniority and the disposition
to vote for spending.[2]

TABLE 5.2   Spending Scores of Senior Representatives
(those serving twelve or more terms)

	Terms served	Spending score
Democrats:		
Jamie L. Whitten (Miss.)	23	32.0
Melvin Price (Ill.)	21	33.0
Charles E. Bennett (Fla.)	19	26.0
Peter W. Rodino, Jr. (N.J.)	19	32.0
Sidney R. Yates (Ill.)	18	35.0
Edward P. Boland (Mass.)	17	32.5
Jack Brooks (Tex.)	17	30.0
William H. Natcher (Ky.)	17	36.0
John D. Dingell (Mich.)	16	33.5
Dante B. Fascell (Fla.)	16	35.5
Jim Wright (Tex.)	16	33.5
Robert W. Kastenmeier (Wis.)	14	32.0
Dan Rostenkowski (Ill.)	14	31.5
Neal Smith (Iowa)	14	33.5
Samuel S. Stratton (N.Y.)	14	29.0
Henry B. Gonzalez (Tex.)	13	34.5
Fernand J. St. Germain (R.I.)	13	31.5
Morris K. Udall (Ariz.)	13	35.5
Don Edwards (Calif.)	12	35.5
Don Fuqua (Fla.)	12	32.5
Sam M. Gibbons (Fla.)	12	20.0
Augustus F. Hawkins (Calif.)	12	34.0
Claude Pepper (Fla.)	12	35.5
J. J. (Jake) Pickle (Tex.)	12	19.5
Edward R. Roybal (Calif.)	12	34.5
Average, senior Democrats		31.9
Average, rest of Democrats		29.6
Republicans:		
William S. Broomfield (Mich.)	15	10.5
Robert H. Michel (Ill.)	15	5.5
Silvio O. Conte (Mass.)	14	32.0
Delbert L. Latta (Ohio)	14	4.0
Frank J. Horton (N.Y.)	12	34.0
Joseph M. McDade (Penn.)	12	27.0
James H. Quillen (Tenn.)	12	18.0
Average, senior Republicans		18.7
Average, rest of Republicans		9.6

NOTE: The respective samples are: senior Democrats, 25; rest of Democrats, 217; senior Republicans, 7; rest of Republicans, 165.

The reasoning behind the seniority test assumed that all representatives enter Congress completely unaffected by any prior prospending persuasion. Clearly, this assumption would often be unjustified. In many cases, before entering Congress the legislator occupied some other post that exposed him to one-sided persuasion. Some have been administrative assistants to other congressmen, for example, and would have been fully exposed to prospending persuasion. Many have been in state legislatures—where, one can assume, one-sided cultures of spending are also at work. Others may have served in state and federal administrative posts, or in local government positions where they were subject to some degree of one-sided persuasion on spending.

It would be expected that these former office-holders would show a greater tendency to vote for spending than the "unsocialized" members who were not exposed to unusual prospending stimuli before entering Congress. To check on this idea, I classified the representatives according to whether or not they held previous government offices. Included in the category of "no prior office" are those who may have held nonpolicy government jobs such as in the military, teaching in state institutions, or as judges or prosecutors. Political party posts were also treated as nonpolicy jobs where the occupant was unlikely to be exposed to significant prospending persuasion.

This effect of prior exposure to spending persuasion should be most evident among the more junior congressmen, of course. After a number of years of service in Congress, the persuasion taking place in that body should tend to even out any differences based on earlier backgrounds. The data for testing this idea are presented in Table 5.3. They support the theory: When they first enter Congress, legislators with prior exposure to prospending persuasion are more in favor of spending.

The seniority effect shown in Table 5.1, although offering some support for the hypothesized persuasion effect, is not conclusive, for it does not show that *being in Congress* is what makes the more senior members more prospending. It is conceivable, for example, that in more recent years entering Congressmen have been more fiscally conservative, whereas the congressmen entering years ago were more liberal to start with and have simply stayed that way.

To check on this possibility, we need to do a longitudinal study of congressmen over time to see what happens to their views. In

TABLE 5.3   The Effect of Prior Governmental Office on Representatives'
Spending (one or two terms' tenure)

	Average spending score	
	Democrats	Republicans
Representatives without prior governmental office	27.3	6.6
Representatives with prior governmental office	29.0	8.5

NOTE: The number of cases in each group respectively is Democrats: 13, 54; Republicans: 16, 39

making this analysis we need a set of congressional spending scores
for many years so that we can track the congressmen for a period of
time. For this purpose, we can use the NTU ratings which, as noted
above, give a close approximation to the nonmilitary spending measure I have developed.

The congressmen selected for analysis are those elected to the
House of Representatives in 1975 and 1977, and who continued to
serve for at least ten years thereafter. In recording their spending
scores, we do not use their absolute NTU scores, for the NTU averages vary from year to year. Instead, I express each congressman's
spending score as a deviation from the average score for his party in
that year. With this method, a score of zero means the congressman's
spending score was the same as the average for his entire party that
year; a positive score means he was a bigger spender than average
for his party; and a negative score means he was less in favor of
spending than his party. Since this method of scoring eliminates the
differences between the parties, it permits combining Democrats
and Republicans in the same tabulation.

The results of this analysis are presented in Figure 5.1, with the
congressmen separated into those with, and those without, prior
government office-holding experience. The results clearly confirm
the culture-of-spending hypothesis. When congressmen first enter
Congress, they are less in favor of spending than their colleagues,
but they grow more in favor of spending as their service in Congress
lengthens. This effect is very large for those congressmen not exposed to culture-of-spending persuasion before entering Congress;
for those who held prior offices, the effect is much weaker.

When we turn to the Senate, we find it somewhat more difficult
to demonstrate the seniority effect. The main problem is that most of

FIGURE 5.1 The Effect of Congressional Tenure on Representatives' Spending

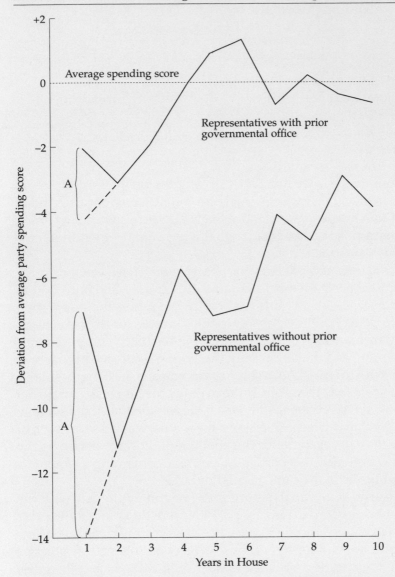

NOTE: Based on Representatives entering Congress in 1975 and 1977 who completed at least ten years of service. The total number of cases in "prior governmental office" category is 46 (37 Democrats and 9 Republicans); in "no prior office" category 13 (9 Democrats and 4 Republicans).
A. Apprenticeship effect (see text).

the senators have had considerable prior exposure to prospending persuasion. Fully one-third have been U.S. representatives, and another one-third have been state legislators, governors, or lieutenant governors.

If we confine our attention to those few senators without prior government office, however, we can see the indoctrination effect at work. Elected to the Senate in 1976, 1978, and 1980 were nine senators who had not held a prior government office, and for whom valid NTU spending scores are available for the six years following their election. These scores are processed in the same way that we tabulated those for the representatives, shown in Figure 5.1, comparing the senator's spending score to the average score for his party (in the Senate, of course). The results are graphed in Figure 5.2, which shows the same general result as that obtained for the representatives: the "unsocialized" senators start out being less in favor of spending than existing senators, and grow more inclined to vote for spending the longer they are immersed in the prevailing one-sided persuasion in favor of spending.

Persuasion and Party Differences

As noted earlier, on the subject of spending there is a substantial difference between the parties, with the Democrats being much more in favor of spending. Using our measurement based on voting in the House of Representatives in 1986, the average spending score for the Democrats is 29.8 and for Republicans, 10.0. How do we account for this difference?

One answer is that the parties have a difference in underlying perspectives that leads to different voting on spending. This is the "ideological theory" we shall take up in the next chapter. Before we turn to this approach, however, we should note that persuasion theory will to some extent account for the gap. Certain persuasion effects strike the parties differently, pushing Democrats to favor spending more than Republicans.

Composition effects. The parties differ somewhat in the characteristics that affect susceptibility to prospending persuasion. First, the Democrats have more senior members. In the 1986 House membership, 52 percent of the Democrats had served five terms or more, but only

FIGURE 5.2   The Effect of Congressional Tenure on Senators' Spending

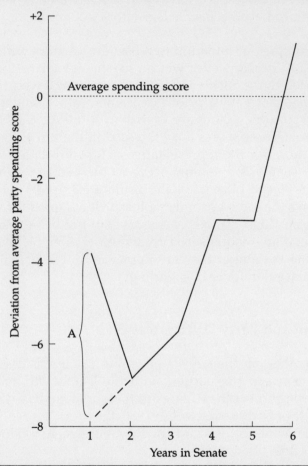

NOTE: Based on Senators entering in 1977, 1979, and 1981 who served for at least six full years and who had not served in other governmental office before entering the Senate. The total number of cases is 9 (2 Democrats and 7 Republicans).
A. Apprenticeship effect (see text).

33 percent of the Republicans had served this long. The Democrats are also slightly more likely to come from governmental backgrounds: In the same 1986 group of representatives, 80 percent of the Democrats had held prior government office, compared to 72 percent of the Republicans. On the basis of membership composition, then, we would expect the Democrats to be the more prospend-

ing party. It has more senior and more "experienced" members who have had longer exposure to prospending persuasion.

Leadership effects. Congressmen are sensitive to their fellow legislators, wanting to "get along" and therefore being willing to "go along." This principle would apply to all types of voting behavior, including voting on spending measures. On such votes, therefore, they would be influenced by more senior, leadership members, especially the leaders in their own party.

One sign of this effect has already cropped up in our data. In Figures 5.1 and 5.2 we notice that the year in which new legislators are most fiscally conservative is not their first year in office, but their second. There clearly seems to be an *apprenticeship effect* at work. In the first year, the congressman is new to the situation, rather insecure, and looks to his party's leaders for cues on how to behave. His own inclinations are to be rather more fiscally conservative than his party, but he is drawn toward more prospending voting by his desire to conform. In the second year, the legislator's insecurities have considerably abated, and he is therefore more inclined to express his more conservative orientation in his voting. Thereafter, he is moved in a prospending direction by the effect of one-sided persuasion.

The size of this apprenticeship effect is indicated in Figures 5.1 and 5.2 by the dotted line that extends the overall trend back to the first year. This projection indicates what the congressman's voting would likely be if there were no apprenticeship effect drawing him toward the bigger-spending party leadership. As the reader can see, this effect is quite substantial for legislators who have not served in other government offices.

Although the effect of leadership weakens after the first year, we may presume that it still exists to some degree in subsequent years. This effect will always be a prospending effect, since the leaders in both parties are the more senior legislators, more in favor of spending (see Table 5.2). The parties seem to differ in the impact of this prospending leadership, however. In the Republican party, there is not a large cadre of senior leaders to begin with, and these leaders are rather mixed in their attitudes toward spending. Furthermore, Republicans are usually the minority party (always in the House, almost always in the Senate), and therefore the party leadership has few carrots or sticks to control the behavior of junior members.

In the Democratic party, these factors are reversed, especially in the House of Representatives. The party has a large senior leadership cadre there. This group is strongly committed to spending, loyal to the federal programs it has built up and supervised over the decades. As majority party leaders, they control the fortunes of the more junior members of their party, deciding on their committee appointments, on many perquisites, and giving or withholding attention for their personal legislative projects. Therefore, the pressures on a junior Democratic legislator to go along with his party leadership on spending are more substantial. One sign that these speculations are correct is seen in the apprenticeship effect. This tendency for beginning congressmen to deviate toward the pro-spending stance of party leaders is much stronger for Democrats than for Republicans.[3]

Another leadership effect concerns the president. Legislators of the president's party tend to support his views, whereas legislators of the opposing party may oppose his positions just to "oppose." In our study period, the Republican president, Reagan, urged opposition to spending on a number of nonmilitary issues, so that we might expect Republicans to vote more against spending and Democrats to favor spending.

Although some such effect of presidential leadership is probably at work, it should not be exaggerated. First, on most spending votes, there is no known presidential position, so that legislators have no guidance on this score. Second, on some (nonmilitary) issues President Reagan announced a *prospending* position, yet even so the Republicans voted against the spending (and the Democrats voted for it).[4]

Feedback effects. In policy communications, like tends to communicate with like. Constituents and lobbyists with a particular message seek out legislators who will give their point a receptive hearing. This pattern will lead to differences in prospending persuasion that would enlarge party differences on spending. The Republicans are known as the opponents of spending, and therefore would be more likely to attract antispending communications. The Democrats, perceived as big spenders, would be shunned by opponents of spending and would more strongly attract lobbyists who urge more spending.

One view of the feedback effect comes from the case of Senator William Proxmire of Wisconsin. In several books about his career, the senator has given a candid account of the evolution of his position on spending. At the beginning of his career, in the 1950s, he was not a conservative, nor did he have any philosophical objection to big government. Indeed, at the same time he was campaigning against government spending, he also proposed massive increases in government programs. Mocking his high-spending proposals in 1958, then–Vice President Richard Nixon labeled him "35-billion Bill"—when $35 billion was real money.[5]

Proxmire adopted the frugality theme, as he reports, mainly because he found constituents responded to an antispending theme. It was a way for him, a "carpetbagger" in Wisconsin, to "identify" with the locals.[6] Once he placed himself visibly on the antispending side, he attracted those who wished to oppose spending, both military and nonmilitary: whistleblowers, cranky constituents, and antispending spokesmen. At the same time, this image of fiscal conservatism tended to repel many prospending lobbyists. I asked one of his former aides about this effect:

Q: Being with that [antispending] image, was he [Proxmire] sought out less by groups that wanted spending?

R: Yes. *(Laughs.)* It was wonderful! We had to put up with relatively few lobbyists coming around, trying to get something for programs.

In effect, Senator Proxmire's stance against spending appears to have created something of an *antispending* subculture for him, as the few antispending activists in Washington singled him out as a receptive audience. The effects of this persuasion seem evident in his voting record. By the mid-1970s, when the NTU began its rating system, Proxmire had become one of the more fiscally conservative senators. This evolution can also be seen in his writings. In his 1972 book, *Uncle Sam—Last of the Bigtime Spenders*, the antispending message was matched by a considerable volume of proposals for new programs and more spending. In his 1980 book, *The Fleecing of America*, the advocacy of spending proposals had shrunk almost to the vanishing point. It must be remembered that Proxmire was a Democrat, so in undergoing this evolution toward being a *relative* antispender, he went against the grain of his party.

It seems possible, then, that feedback effects could be a factor in the difference between the parties on spending. Compared to Democrats, Republicans probably get fewer prospending communications and more antispending communications. The magnitude of this effect is probably quite small, however, given the small number of antispending voices generally present in Washington. Even for Republicans, the overwhelming majority of communications on specific spending programs will be in favor of spending.

Conclusion

In addition to providing support for the culture-of-spending theory, these findings about the effect of prospending indoctrination suggest certain political reforms that would help limit spending. One is the limitation of congressional terms. Since longer service in Congress disposes legislators to be more in favor of spending, limiting these terms would result in a more fiscally conservative Congress. This issue is discussed at length in Chapter 11. Another reform that would have similar effect is a limit on prior office holding. If, let us say, former representatives were barred from the Senate, or if former state legislators were barred from both houses, our figures indicate that a more fiscally conservative Congress would result. Needless to say, there would be political and constitutional objections to such reforms, but they at least serve to illustrate the kind of institutional changes that the persuasion theory of spending suggests.

✦ 6 ✦

Party, Ideology, and Spending

IN THE LAST CHAPTER, we noted the existence of a substantial difference between the parties on spending, with Democrats being more prospending than Republicans. The usual way of accounting for this difference is to refer to a difference in ideology, along the following lines. The Democrats, it would be said, are the traditional left-wing party, seeking to use the powers of government to enhance the condition of the "have-nots" in society. As a result, they vote for (nonmilitary) spending measures because these measures are, in effect, redistributionist: They shift money from the wealthy to the underprivileged in the form of health care, food benefits, retirement benefits, educational benefits, and so forth. The Republicans are presumed to represent the "haves" in society. As a classic "right-wing" party, they would be expected to oppose most government programs because they seek to protect the wealth of their middle- and upper-class supporters.

It may well be that in the past this lineup of the parties on the ideological front did exist, at least in rough terms, but in the modern era this traditional ideological picture no longer applies. We still use the terms "left" and "right" and we still apply them to the parties in the traditional way, but beneath the labels, a considerable transformation of their meaning has occurred.

I first became aware of the inapplicability of the old concepts when I started looking at the actual spending bills. I recommend this experience to anyone who would advance theories about why congressmen vote for spending measures: Pick up some volumes of

Congressional Quarterly and inspect the actual content of the different spending measures. One of the first things you will notice is that the overwhelming majority of spending measures have nothing to do with redistribution, nothing to do with benefits targeted for the poor and underprivileged.

The point stands out clearly in the thirty-six spending votes figuring in the 1986 spending measure introduced in the previous chapter, a representative sample of the spending bills on which a split vote occurred. Of this collection of votes, there are, even by generous count, only ten that could be placed in the "redistribution/antipoverty" category. These include votes on spending levels for migrant health centers, Indian housing, the Departments of Labor, Health and Human Services, and Education, public housing, the Legal Services Corporation, and VISTA. A skeptic would point out that there is considerable nonpoor interest even in these measures, but let us accept them as genuine antipoverty measures.

These votes constitute less than one-third of all the votes in the sample. For the other twenty-six spending votes, there either are no clear beneficiaries, or the immediate beneficiaries are middle- or upper-class individuals. They include votes on spending levels for the Departments of Commerce, of Justice, of State, the Treasury, the Post Office, for the Consumer Product Safety Commission, for energy-research projects, for water projects, for Amtrak, for the Los Angeles subway, for a salinity-research laboratory, for agricultural subsidies, for law-enforcement agencies, for a commission on collegiate athletics, for legislative branch appropriations, for aid to the Philippines, for the development of Columbia River Gorge, for urban development grants, for small business loans, and even funding to study bubonic plague.

In the main, federal domestic spending is *not* spending on the poor. Many observers have made this point, so that one would think it ought to be common knowledge by now.[1] Somehow, this reality keeps getting overlooked when the ideology of spending is under discussion.

Given this fact about the character of spending bills, how would old-fashioned liberals vote on spending? The broad prediction is that they would *not* be big spenders. They would vote for antipoverty spending. They would vote against spending going to middle- and upper-class beneficiaries, and they should exhibit a rather mixed, undefined pattern on general, nonbeneficiary spending (such as the funding of the State Department, and so forth).

This is not what happens. The Democrats do indeed vote strongly for antipoverty spending. That much fits the old image. *They also vote just as strongly for all other types of (nonmilitary) spending, including measures that have no redistributionist implications, and even for measures whose beneficiaries are clearly middle- and upper-income groups.*

Let us take a few examples from the 1986 House votes used to calculate the spending score. The bill on enhancing the Columbia River Gorge was approved by 97 percent of the Democrats and only 47 percent of the Republicans. The bill to create an advisory commission on collegiate athletics was approved by 84 percent of the Democrats and only 26 percent of the Republicans. The measure to provide a higher level of general Treasury and Post Office funding was supported by 49 percent of the Democrats and only 18 percent of the Republicans. The bill to establish a salinity laboratory was approved by 97 percent of the Democrats and only 55 percent of the Republicans. The measure for higher Amtrak funding was supported by 82 percent of the Democrats and only 28 percent of the Republicans. Spending for Urban Action Development Grants (scorned by many as subsidies to well-heeled corporations) was supported by 95 percent of the Democrats and only 48 percent of the Republicans.

This same point about consistency in the support for all types of domestic spending is made in different form in Appendix Table A1, where the voting for the different types of spending are correlated against each other. The results show that voting for one type of (nonmilitary) spending is positively associated with voting for *every other type of nonmilitary spending*.

Does this finding mean that Democrats are no longer left-wing? The answer depends on how one defines "left." If we are speaking of traditional left-wingers, the answer would appear to be affirmative: Old-fashioned redistributionists have disappeared from the American political scene. What has happened, however, is that the application of "left," and its modern synonym "liberal," has shifted along with the change in the behavior of congressional Democrats, so that "liberal" today applies to those congressmen who vote for all kinds of (nonmilitary) spending, including spending for the middle class, the well-to-do, and subsidies for businesses.

A direct way to demonstrate this point is to employ the rankings of Americans for Democratic Action, considered to be the quintessential "liberal" organization. It rates congressmen each year on the basis of how they voted on key measures, and the results are taken by scholars and the media to be an authoritative "liberalism" score.

Not surprisingly, the ADA ratings show that the Democrats are the left-wing party: Their House members have an average liberalism score of 69, compared to an average rating of 14 for the Republicans. (A score of 100 is highest; zero is lowest.) It is less well known, however, that ADA ratings are an almost perfect predictor of a legislator's general disposition to support domestic spending measures of any kind—the higher the ADA score, the more of a spender the congressman will be. One demonstration of this point is to cross-tabulate the ADA scores against our spending scores, as shown in Table 6.1:

TABLE 6.1   Relationship between Representatives' ADA Liberalism Rating and Nonmilitary Spending Scores

ADA Liberalism rating	Average spending score
0 to 29	8.9
30 to 69	24.9
70 to 100	32.1

NOTE: The number of representatives in the respective categories is as follows: ADA ratings of 0 to 29, 157; 30 to 69, 101; 70 to 100, 156.

The point can be further demonstrated by inspecting the relation between ADA liberalism scores and support for pro-business spending. In the traditional ideological paradigm, the "left" is supposed to be squarely opposed to government spending for businesses. In the first place, such spending redistributes wealth in the *wrong* direction, in favor of the well-to-do. Furthermore, the left is traditionally skeptical of private business as "selfish" and "exploitative."

Among the thirty-six spending votes that figure in our 1986 House spending scale, four were quite clearly pro-business spending measures (the numbers in parentheses refer to Congressional Quarterly 1986 roll-call votes):

- A measure to establish a trust fund to compensate companies deemed to be harmed by imports (CQ 121);
- Funding for the Urban Development Action Grant (UDAG) program (CQ 130). Under this program, money is lent at favorable rates to contractors and corporations, including Hyatt, Holiday Inn, and Hilton, to build commercial structures such as luxury hotels.

- Funding for the Economic Development Administration (EDA) in the Department of Commerce, which funds private development projects such as golf courses, marinas, and tourist attractions (CQ 204).
- Funding for loans to nondisadvantaged small businesses (CQ 207). Specifically exempted from this attempt to cut back SBA loans were loans for minority-owned businesses and other businesses deemed to be "disadvantaged." Hence, the congressmen were voting on subsidized loans to ordinary small businesses.

These four votes form a "pro-business spending" subscore of our spending score, identifying programs that have been denounced by journalists as welfare-for-the-rich spending.[2] How did congressional liberals vote on these pro-business spending measures? Table 6.2 lists the forty-five congressmen who obtained the extremely high ADA rating of 95 and 100. As the reader can see, these pure "liberals," all of whom happen to be Democrats, strongly supported pro-business spending. The overwhelming majority voted for all four pro-business spending measures. Only two of these forty-five congressmen voted against pro-business spending even once. (Since a missed vote is given a score of 0.5, a score of 3.5 means the congressman voted three times for pro-business spending and was absent once.)

As the tabulation of total spending scores in Table 6.2 shows, those congressmen with extremely high ADA ratings are big spenders in general. That is, these congressmen are voting for the full range of (nonmilitary) spending programs, programs that span the gamut of beneficiaries, from poor to rich, from underprivileged to overprivileged.

The tabulation in Table 6.3 shows that those congressmen whom the ADA rates at the bottom of its scale, at zero, represent the opposite position on spending. They are all Republicans, and opposed the pro-business spending. In fact, not one of these forty-three "conservative" congressman voted for a majority of the pro-business spending measures, and the overwhelming majority opposed all four. This outcome will surprise anyone reasoning from the traditional ideological categories, because in that framework "conservatives" are supposed to be friendly toward businessmen, and are

TABLE 6.2 Voting of Liberals on Business Subsidies, Amtrak Spending, and Law-Enforcement Funding (1986 Representatives with ADA rating of ninety-five and over)

	1986 ADA rating	1986 spending score[a]	Pro-business spending[b]	Vote for higher Amtrak spending	Vote for law-enforcement funding
Robert T. Matsui (Calif.)	95	35.0	4.0	yes	yes
Ronald V. Dellums (Calif.)	100	34.5	3.0	yes	yes
Fortney H. (Pete) Stark (Calif.)	95	34.0	4.0	yes	yes
Don Edwards (Calif.)	100	35.5	4.0	yes	yes
Norman Y. Mineta (Calif.)	95	36.0	4.0	yes	yes
Henry A. Waxman (Calif.)	95	33.5	4.0	yes	yes
Edward R. Roybal (Calif.)	95	34.5	3.5	yes	yes
Howard L. Berman (Calif.)	95	31.5	3.5	yes	yes
Mervyn M. Dymally (Calif.)	100	35.5	3.5	yes	yes
George E. Brown, Jr. (Calif.)	95	35.5	3.5	yes	yes
Patricia Schroeder (Colo.)	95	29.0	4.0	yes	yes
Samuel Gedjenson (Conn.)	95	32.0	4.0	yes	yes
William Lehman (Fla.)	100	35.0	4.0	yes	no
Charles A. Hayes (Ill.)	95	34.0	3.5	yes	yes
Gus Savage (Ill.)	95	34.0	3.5	yes	yes
Cardiss Collins (Ill.)	95	32.0	3.5	yes	yes
Lane Evans (Ill.)	100	32.5	4.0	yes	yes
Steny H. Hoyer (Md.)	95	35.5	4.0	yes	yes
Barney Frank (Mass.)	100	31.0	4.0	yes	yes
Edward J. Markey (Mass.)	95	30.5	4.0	yes	—
Gerry E. Studds (Mass.)	95	35.0	4.0	yes	yes
Dale E. Kildee (Mich.)	95	36.0	4.0	yes	yes

TABLE 6.2 *(continued)*

	1986 ADA rating	1986 spend- ing score[a]	Pro- business spending[b]	Vote for higher Amtrak spending	Vote for law- enforcement funding
David E. Bonior (Mich.)	95	33.5	3.0	yes	yes
George Crockett, Jr. (Mich.)	95	32.0	4.0	yes	yes
Martin Olav Sabo (Minn.)	95	35.0	4.0	yes	no
Alan Wheat (Mo.)	95	34.0	4.0	yes	yes
Peter W. Rodino, Jr. (N.J.)	100	32.0	3.0	yes	yes
Thomas J. Downey (N.Y.)	95	33.0	4.0	yes	yes
James H. Scheuer (N.Y.)	95	34.0	4.0	yes	yes
Edolphus Towns (N.Y.)	95	34.5	3.5	yes	yes
Major R. Owens (N.Y.)	95	34.5	4.0	yes	yes
Charles B. Rangel (N.Y.)	100	34.5	3.5	yes	yes
Ted Weiss (N.Y.)	95	32.5	4.0	yes	yes
Robert Garcia (N.Y.)	95	34.5	3.5	yes	yes
Henry J. Nowak (N.Y.)	95	34.5	4.0	yes	yes
James A. Traficant, Jr. (Ohio)	95	35.0	4.0	yes	yes
Edward F. Feighan (Ohio)	95	30.5	4.0	yes	yes
Mary Rose Oakar (Ohio)	95	36.0	4.0	yes	yes
Louis Stokes (Ohio)	100	34.5	4.0	yes	no
William J. Coyne (Penn.)	100	35.5	4.0	yes	yes
Harold E. Ford (Tenn.)	100	31.5	4.0	—	yes
Mickey Leland (Tex.)	100	36.0	4.0	yes	yes
Henry B. Gonzalez (Tex.)	100	34.5	4.0	yes	no
Mike Lowry (Wash.)	95	34.5	4.0	yes	no
Robert Kastenmeier (Wis.)	100	32.0	4.0	yes	no

a. Maximum = 36.
b. Maximum = 4.

TABLE 6.3 Voting of Conservatives on Business Subsidies, Amtrak
Spending, and Law-Enforcement Funding (1986
Representatives with ADA rating of zero)

	1986 ADA rating	1986 spend-ing score[a]	Pro-business spending[b]	Vote for higher Amtrak spending	Vote for law-enforcement funding
H. L. (Sonny) Callahan (Ala.)	0	6.5	1.0	no	no
Bob Stump (Ariz.)	0	1.0	0.0	no	no
Norman D. Shumway (Calif.)	0	1.0	0.0	no	no
Carlos J. Moorehead (Calif.)	0	3.0	0.0	no	no
David Dreier (Calif.)	0	2.0	0.0	no	no
Jerry Lewis (Calif.)	0	15.5	1.0	yes	no
Robert E. Badham (Calif.)	0	4.0	0.5	no	no
Dan E. Lungren (Calif.)	0	1.0	0.0	no	no
Duncan L. Hunter (Calif.)	0	7.0	1.0	no	—
Dan Schaefer (Colo.)	0	5.0	0.0	yes	no
Bill McCollum (Fla.)	0	6.0	0.0	no	no
Andy Ireland (Fla.)	0	3.5	1.0	no	no
Connie Mack (Fla.)	0	1.0	0.5	no	no
Patrick L. Swindall (Ga.)	0	2.0	0.0	no	no
Newt Gingrich (Ga.)	0	3.5	0.0	no	no
Philip M. Crane (Ill.)	0	1.5	0.5	no	no
Edward R. Madigan (Ill.)	0	15.0	2.0	yes	no
John P. Hiler (Ind.)	0	2.0	0.0	no	no
Pat Roberts (Kan.)	0	3.0	0.0	no	no
Robert L. (Bob) Livingston (La.)	0	10.5	2.0	yes	no
Marjorie S. Holt (Md.)	0	14.5	2.0	yes	no

TABLE 6.3 *(continued)*

	1986 ADA rating	1986 spending score[a]	Pro-business spending[b]	Vote for higher Amtrak spending	Vote for law-enforcement funding
Mark D. Siljander (Mich.)	0	4.5	0.0	no	no
Guy Vander Jagt (Mich.)	0	7.0	1.5	no	yes
Ron Marlenee (Mont.)	0	7.5	0.0	yes	no
Barbara F. Vucanovich (Nev.)	0	9.0	2.0	no	no
Robert C. Smith (N.H.)	0	1.0	0.0	no	no
Gerald B. H. Solomon (N.Y.)	0	9.5	2.0	no	yes
Fred J. Eckert (N.Y.)	0	1.0	0.0	no	no
Michael G. Oxley (Ohio)	0	1.0	0.0	no	no
Michael DeWine (Ohio)	0	7.0	1.0	yes	no
Denny Smith (Ore.)	0	1.0	0.0	no	no
Robert S. Walker (Penn.)	0	0.0	0.0	no	no
Joe L. Barton (Tenn.)	0	3.0	0.0	no	no
Bill Archer (Tex.)	0	1.5	0.0	no	no
Jack Fields (Tex.)	0	3.0	0.0	no	no
Thomas D. DeLay (Tex.)	0	3.5	0.0	no	no
Richard K. Armey (Tex.)	0	0.0	0.0	no	no
James V. Hansen (Utah)	0	2.0	1.0	no	no
David S. Monson (Utah)	0	2.5	0.5	no	no
Herbert H. Bateman (Va.)	0	14.0	2.0	no	no
D. French Slaughter (Va.)	0	4.5	0.0	yes	no
Toby Roth (Wis.)	0	8.5	2.5	no	no
Richard B. Cheney (Wyo.)	0	3.0	0.0	no	no

a. Maximum = 36.
b. Maximum = 4.

presumed to favor the idea of diverting government monies to their well-to-do supporters.

Another spending issue involving perverse income transfer is Amtrak funding. There would seem to be no antipoverty element in this federal program of rail-passenger subsidy. The workers are well-paid and middle class, and the riders are middle class, too. As an editor of the *New Republic* put it, the Amtrak subsidy exists "mainly to guarantee the upper middle class trains in the Boston to Washington corridor. This is class legislation of the worst sort."[3] In 1986, the House voted on a proposal to hold Amtrak funding at $591 million, the previous year's level, rather than increasing the subsidy by $22 million (CQ 241). Table 6.2 shows how the ideal "liberals" voted on this "class legislation of the worst sort": Forty-four out of forty-five voted for *higher funding* for Amtrak, and the forty-fifth congressman was absent. As shown in Table 6.3, it was the "conservatives," with zero ADA ratings, who overwhelmingly opposed the higher Amtrak subsidy.

Another indication of the irrelevance of the old ideological categories is the behavior of the two groups toward federal grants to state and local law-enforcement agencies (CQ 341). Traditionally, the left has opposed the idea of beefing up police forces on the grounds that police action ("oppression," "brutality") typically takes place against the poor. As the reader can see in Table 6.2, the traditional pattern is squarely contradicted: The "liberals" voted overwhelmingly in favor of increased law-enforcement grants. Table 6.3 shows that the standard categories are equally inapplicable for "conservatives." Traditionally, conservatives are supposed to be strong supporters of the police as defenders of property and the established order; yet these modern "conservatives" voted overwhelmingly against the increased spending for law-enforcement agencies.

The findings just given have constituted a simple truth about American politics for the past decade, readily apparent to anyone who cared to examine congressional voting patterns. Even as far back as the Chrysler bailout of 1979, the pattern was clear, with the Democrats strongly supporting, and the Republicans opposing, this federal subsidy for the benefit of corporate stockholders, management, and highly paid auto workers.[4] Nevertheless, even a decade later, this transformation of the ideological landscape is still not generally appreciated. Reporters continue to portray Republicans as supporters of pro-business spending even when the actual roll-call votes contradict their allegations.[5]

A New Ideology?

The traditional left-right ideological categories do not underlie the party split on spending. At the same time, there is a consistent pattern in the voting on spending. To avoid confusion, it would be helpful to identify this different pattern with a different term: I have chosen "N-liberal," to indicate that the position is popularly called "liberal" and seems to trace its ancestry from views formerly called "liberal," but is something rather different, and also new (hence "N"). In the same way, we can label the opponents of these new liberals "N-conservatives."

The main feature of the N-liberal position is the broad support of *all* types of (nonmilitary) government spending programs, regardless of the nature of their beneficiaries. A second ingredient, which we shall examine in Chapter 8, is an opposition to military spending. N-liberals and N-conservatives also have distinctive views on a number of other points, including nuclear power and other technological risks, democratic procedural reform, foreign involvement, the regulation of business and commerce, and race relations. We shall not explore these aspects, since such an examination would take us rather far afield, but they should be noted to complete the picture.

How does one account for N-liberal ideology, especially as it bears on government spending? What are its organizing principles? One possibility is that N-liberals are motivated by a pro-government bias, even a disposition to worship the state. This would account for their consistent support of government programs, regardless of beneficiary. If they believed that government was a wonderful institution, that anything it did was ipso facto right and good, this would account for their behavior.

This idea is contradicted by the opposition of N-liberals to military spending. Military forces are one of the most visible elements of state power, a type of spending that state-worshippers, especially, would support. Another point that doesn't fit this "state-worshipping" theory is the lack of concern with government size. Politicians who explicitly believe in government would want to see it grow, taking over more and more functions. When I asked N-liberal congressmen and their spokesmen about state size and governmental growth, I found they were not interested in the subject. They saw no virtue in "big government" as such.

The "state-worship" idea, then, seems unconvincing. The growth of the federal government has been a by-product of the behavior of N-liberals, not its aim.

As I talked further with aides and congressmen, I began to wonder if a systematic world view underlies the N-liberal position. As I pressed them to give their explanations for why this or that spending program was desirable, the answers were ad hoc. They defended each program as good in and of itself, without referring to any overall principle. Their support for pro-business spending, for example, was simply explained as a way of helping local economies and improving "the jobs picture."

The argument that the N-liberals use most frequently to justify spending programs is particularly revealing. It is that government spending for the program will *save the government money!* The point may seem ironic, but congressmen take it seriously. Armed with the biased cost–benefit estimates of prospending consultants, administrators, and pressure groups, congressmen make "saving money" a routine argument for spending it: Federal feeding programs save the government money by reducing the medicaid costs that bad nutrition of the poor would otherwise entail, job training saves on unemployment benefits, agricultural subsidies keep farmers from being forced to move to the cities where they would be on welfare, public works projects are net "revenue generators," and so on.

Such arguments, as I explain in the Appendix, "Fallacies of Cost–Benefit Analysis," are not very well grounded, but the fact that they are used so heavily indicates the immediate, practical orientation of the high-spending congressmen. They do not see spending as an ideological issue. Typically, N-liberals reject the label "liberal" and call themselves "issue-oriented" or "pragmatic." They explicitly break with old-fashioned equalitarians and disparage what one called the "Robin Hood complex" of seeking to take from the rich and give to the poor. They like to think of themselves as moving toward the "center" of the political spectrum. Even the word "ideological" has a negative connotation, used disparagingly to refer to someone who resists the group position. Compromising, getting along, being "realistic": These are the congressional virtues exemplified by the N-liberals.

We see this nonideological orientation in the following interview excerpt with this high-spending liberal Democratic congressman from the Northwest (ADA rating 80; spending score 31 out of 36):

Q: Would you describe yourself as a liberal or a conservative?

R: I think all those pigeonholes are pretty much useless today. There are items I am very conservative on, like fighting crime. There are items that I might be . . . by some classic definition, philosophically different on. I think virtually nothing useful is accomplished by these labels.

Q: What about spending for things like business-type spending? Are you in favor of that? Say, like EDA or UDAG?

R: I have supported EDA and UDAG primarily because I think it's been a relatively small program where there have been some significant benefits. Again, I don't try to do anything but look at each expenditure in the light of whether it's cost-effective, whether it's really going to produce benefits that are publicly oriented.

Q: Do you consider yourself a redistributionist, shifting income from wealthier people to poorer people? Are you aiming at that?

R: No. Absolutely not. Again, I think these labels are not. . .

Q: Because liberals would be expected to do that.

R: I don't agree with that either. I see nothing in the definition of "liberal" which automatically says you're for redistributing the wealth. My feeling is that—I'm certainly no arch-conservative, I guess, by anybody's definition—

Q: No. *(laughs)*

R: —is that I'm interested in economic initiatives that increase the pie, that increase wealth. And I also think government should have a heart for the people who are truly incapable of helping themselves. Again, I'm not going to let some label be attached to my name. . . .

I'm going to take steps to increase the pie, to increase wealth in our society, and I'm also for a government that tries to reach out to people who really aren't capable of helping themselves, for two reasons. One, I think it is what a fair and compassionate government ought to do. Second, is that it will usually cost us more if we don't. If we don't help, for example, medicaid recipients, health care in the community, very often they will end up in institutions which will cost far more.

This comment gives a comprehensive picture of the thinking of the high-spending, N-liberal congressman. He sees himself as a pragmatist, using government to do good. His policies, whether helping business or helping the poor, come not from any philosophical theory but from a simple desire for improvement: Spending programs help people, increase the pie, or save money.

What about the N-conservatives? Does their position represent the outgrowth of a systematic philosophy? A number of ideological theories would underlie a general antispending stance. One is the libertarian perspective that emphasizes leaving individuals in freedom, that is, uncoerced by either private or governmental authority. The formal libertarian view is of rather recent vintage, but its roots go back to the perspectives of the Founding Fathers, including Thomas Jefferson and his belief in minimal government. Another, related, philosophy would be the system of laissez-faire economics as propounded by Adam Smith. These worldviews would prompt a congressman to vote rather consistently against government spending of all types.

There are several reasons to doubt, however, that in voting against spending Republicans are applying a systematic ideology. In the first place, we should keep in mind that Republicans are not *that* different from Democrats on spending. My method of constructing the spending score emphasizes differences between congressmen because it employs split votes, that is, votes where at least 20 percent voted on the losing side. The unanimous or nearly unanimous votes in favor of spending are not employed in the scale. Because of this feature, it cannot be said that a Republican who obtained a score of zero was truly against all spending. In most cases, he would have joined the spenders on the nearly unanimous spending votes. He should therefore be considered a moderate, not a low, spender.

The N-conservative Republicans lean against spending, but they are not consistently opposed to it—as would be expected if they were following a systematic ideology.

In my interviews with Republican congressmen and staffers, I heard very few right-wing ideological premises. Like the N-liberals, their approach seemed to be more "practical" than ideological. When challenged about their support of certain kinds of spending, one pointed to the Preamble of the Constitution which looks to government to "promote the general welfare," and another rationalized that 'if I don't spend it for my state, others will spend it for theirs.' When I asked them about libertarianism they explicitly rejected it as too extreme.

This comment by a low-spending Northeast Republican congressman (ADA rating of 5, spending score of 1.0 on the 36-point scale) reflects this pragmatic orientation:

Q: Would you describe yourself as a conservative? I mean, on the spending issue?

R: Absolutely! Yes, Yes. Oh absolutely. You have to conscientiously do that. You have to. Almost on every vote I'll look at it and sometimes it hurts me because sometimes it affects my district. Sometimes it affects a program that I support. But I have to look at it in terms of the whole budget. If I see that it's out of line, I don't support it—because of the budgetary situation we have now. I look down the road at the long run, saying, to be shortsighted, voting more sums of money than we should, which thus causes us to borrow more and eat up more and more in interest [on the national debt], has the snowball effect which costs us more.

This congressman is not opposing spending because it is wrong in principle. He believes that many government programs are good, and he likes the idea of government helping his district. He is tempted by spending—but resists in order to hold down debt and interest payments in the long run.

One of the most common reasons conservative congressmen give for opposing programs is that "it doesn't work." They point to experiences that show that the policy in question either did not solve the problem, or made the problem worse.

For example, I pressed one conservative Republican congressman from the Northwest to explain his opposition to spending programs such as agricultural subsidies. His argument was entirely pragmatic:

R: I watched in the 1960s—and I watched with first-hand knowledge because of our farming and ranching involvement, and also because I was a realtor—I saw young families identify for a Farm Home loan and buy a ranch or a farm at the peak of a market that in no way could cash-flow if the market dropped 5 cents.

> Ten years later those poor folks were bankrupt, they'd
> had a very negative experience. They felt they had been
> wronged badly—not in the first instance: When you're giv-
> ing out money, nobody feels they're wronged. But when you
> fail to continue to give it out, then they feel they're wronged.
> Now that's what I mean in the example of agriculture.

In other words, there is a considerable similarity in the way both
N-liberals and N-conservatives approach the policy world. Both es-
chew philosophical formulations, and both adopt a utilitarian perspective. Even though they have the same practical approach,
however, they often wind up with different conclusions on spending questions. In the following section, I shall attempt to explain
why they weigh the costs and benefits of programs differently.

Or Habit of Mind?

It seems unprofitable to try to explain N-liberal and N-conservative
viewpoints as the outgrowth of a systematic, articulated thought
system. Although some strands of ideological systems can be found
in these perspectives, they are not, in the main, systematic philoso-
phies. Disappointing as this conclusion may be to the academic supporters of either camp, it should not come as a surprise. We are
dealing, after all, with politicians, not political philosophers.

If these positions do not represent intellectual systems, what
causes them? What is the underlying force that brings these two
camps of politicians, each claiming to be pragmatic, to different
positions on spending? There may be a number of answers to this
question; I find the following explanation persuasive.

Many policy questions have a peculiar asymmetry in the arguments that bear on them. The arguments on one side are direct,
immediate, and visible, while the arguments on the other are indirect, theoretical, or even speculative. To take an individual-level
illustration, suppose you are accosted by a beggar asking for money.
What should you do? Let us assume the money involved is trivial,
so the question of self-interest is not at issue. Giving the beggar a
dollar seems like an immediate way of helping. In the long run,
however, this may prove to be harmful, for he may spend the dollar
on alcohol, let us say, further impairing his health.

Both alternatives, giving or not giving, are defensible, but they are not of the same character. Giving the dollar has a "manifest" appeal. It is "helpful" in an immediate sense. The beggar will be, at the moment, grateful. The case for not giving the dollar is future-oriented. It is a course of action that will leave the beggar better off in the long run—if the theory about alcohol abuse is correct. In other words, it involves a "latent" perspective. We can say that issues involving these two different perspectives contain a "manifest/ latent asymmetry." Disagreements on them are caused by a different emphasis on immediate, as opposed to long-run, perspectives.

It seems plausible that politicians vary in the degree to which they emphasize the manifest over the latent. Some may be very affected by the impulse to "do something now," inclined to respond to injuries they can *see* and to ignore problems or suffering that theories say might come later. Others, at the opposite end of the spectrum, stress the long-run, theoretical effects of policies. These two types of politicians would react differently to policy questions involving a manifest/latent asymmetry.

One illustration of a policy issue of this kind is minimum-wage legislation. The problem, as immediately perceived, is that some workers are paid an unfortunately low wage. The immediately attractive solution is to pass a law requiring the payment of a higher wage. Politicians responsive to manifest aspects of policy will favor minimum-wage legislation.

Politicians less affected by immediate considerations will be swayed in the opposite direction. They follow theories that predict that minimum-wage legislation will do harm in the long run. Under one theory, for example, this measure will raise the wage of some unskilled workers above what they are worth, so that they are discharged (or go unhired). If true, this theory means that in the long run, minimum-wage legislation hurts the very workers it is supposed to help.

We would say that the N-liberals represent the type of legislator who is most affected by the immediate aspect of things, and disposed to support the manifest solutions to problems. The N-conservatives tend to discount the manifest, and are more inclined to emphasize the latent aspects of a policy question.

This theory will fit the positions on the minimum wage, which N-liberals support and N-conservatives oppose. It also fits the (new) positions on protectionism. This issue is a classic one involving a manifest/latent asymmetry. The firms and workers who are threatened by imports are known and visible, whereas the benefits of free trade are diffuse and theoretical. Protecting industries from the hardships imposed by foreign competition is therefore the manifestly helpful thing to do. We would expect N-liberals to be protectionist—which in fact is the case. The ADA now includes support for protectionism as a "good" vote in its ratings.[6]

On many policy issues, the application of this manifest/latent theory will be rather ambiguous, given the difficulty one would have in defining which side—if either—represented the manifest one. The main task here, however, is to account for patterns of support for spending. On this point, the theory about different perspectives seems to fit. On spending issues, especially as presented to congressmen in the one-sided way that prevails today, the manifest point of view is that one can do some good by spending, and that one would do harm by cutting programs. Therefore, the congressman disposed to concentrate on the manifest will favor a broad range of helpful-seeming programs: spending for the poor, spending for farmers, spending for businesses, spending for scientists, spending for the arts, and so on.

Opposition to all these government spending programs will come from congressmen who resist the manifest perspective that spending is beneficial. They are congressmen who heed arguments that in the long run the program will fail or cause harm, or who worry more about the effect of the spending on the eventual deficit and its negative economic implications.

Take, for example, a pro-business spending program such as UDAG grants. In a short-run, immediate perspective, a project to build a hotel seems attractive: Workers will be employed, tax revenues will be generated, tourism will be encouraged. A congressman responsive to manifest appearances would vote for such a project. His support does not mean he is "pro-business," or that he is operating from any ideology of "capitalism" or "corporatism." He has simply seen a helpful-seeming program, something that seems to enlarge the economic pie.

The indirect considerations on such a spending program tend to go in the opposite direction. To fund the hotel, for example, tax monies have to be taken from other businesses. As a result, their expansion will be curtailed, with corresponding negative effects on employment, and so forth. A congressman responsive to latent considerations such as these would therefore be inclined to vote against the project. His vote would not reflect any "anti-business" ideology. He simply saw a negative, latent aspect of the program.

This formulation is consistent with how congressmen describe their positions on spending. As noted above, N-conservatives explain their opposition to spending programs mainly on the grounds that they do not work in the long run, or that they add to the deficit and the interest charges that in the long run will burden the budget. The N-liberals are less inclined to weigh such long-run considerations. They focus, simply, on the immediate problem to be solved. A conservative Republican senator described this orientation (and, by implication, his own disposition to weigh latent aspects) when I asked him how he accounted for the "really energetic spenders":

R: Some people are just compulsive do-gooders. They like to do good things and the fact that there's an adverse effect to it, [they say] "Well, we'll take care of that later. Let's just do this good thing now." And a lot of that means government programs of some kind. People are hungry, they need food, let's feed them. No matter what it costs or how you get it. People have medical needs, we'll create a program to meet their medical needs. Don't worry about what it costs, we'll deal with that somehow else. People need welfare of any form? Well, let's meet that need, no matter. We won't worry about the consequences of that action. We'll deal with consequences later.

This, then, is my interpretation of the party split on spending. The Democrats—the N-liberals—have a relatively high proportion of legislators inclined to emphasize the manifest aspect of policies. This is an impulse that leads them to favor immediate government solutions to apparent problems. The Republicans—who tend to be N-conservatives—are more disposed to emphasize latent aspects of policies. They are more inclined to weigh the long-run costs or harm of a government program, and are therefore less enthusiastic about funding it.

Accounting for the connections between party, ideology, and spending is a difficult problem, especially since even the elementary facts about *who* is supporting *which* spending are still controversial. My aim here has not been to advance conclusive answers, but to begin working toward an explanation.

✦ 7 ✦

Electoral Theories of Spending

IN OUR SURVEY OF EXPLANATIONS for why congressmen favor spending, there remains one major theory to evaluate. This is the idea that congressmen are forced to vote for spending by the operation of the democratic electoral system. This view is undeniably popular. When I would mention to friends and acquaintances that I was writing a book to explain why congressmen support spending, I was repeatedly told that my study was quite unnecessary since the answer to my question was already well known: "It's obvious, isn't it?" they would say. "They want to get reelected."

One can hardly find a criticism of spending practices in Washington that does not trace the problem to elections. For example, a *Wall Street Journal* editorial criticizing a House vote supporting water projects declared:

> It is now clear that whatever else they once may have thought to be their broader responsibilities as elected federal officials, congressional delegations are now driven by one, narrow imperative: to survive their 1986 elections.[1]

A political scientist adopts the same perspective in explaining the rise of the welfare state:

> The existence of the Washington system locks us into the New Deal way of doing things: Pass a law, appropriate a lot of money, and establish a new federal bureaucracy. No reasoned

113

analysis underlies that method of operation. The electoral interest of incumbent congressmen does.[2]

When examined closely, the notion that elections cause congressmen to spend is not a single theory, but a family of ideas. We shall
look at two main variants of the theme, the "economic voter" and the
"image protection" theories. These by no means exhaust the possibilities, but they serve as a useful introduction to the issues involved.

The Economic-Voter Theory

Perhaps the most popular version of the spending-voting connection is what might be termed the "economic-voter" theory. In this
view, voters want government spending for themselves. In order to
please these voters, and be elected and reelected by them, congressmen vote for the respective spending programs. Voters in general
may be opposed to this "special interest" spending, but they don't
know about it, or it is too small in the overall spending picture to
matter to them, so it does not influence their electoral behavior.
Hence the congressman ensures his reelection by constantly voting
for more and more spending.

The classic illustration of this pattern is thought to be the voting
for farm subsidies. The handful of farmers want them, but the rest
of the voters don't really care one way or the other. According to the
theory, it is always in the congressman's electoral interest to support
subsidies.

Former budget director David Stockman summarizes this theory in addressing the possibility that voters have a general antispending philosophy:

> The actual electorate, however, is not interested in this doctrine;
> when it is interested at all, it is interested in getting help from
> the government to compensate for a perceived disadvantage.
> Consequently, the spending politics of Washington do reflect
> the heterogeneous and parochial demands that arise from the
> diverse, activated fragments of the electorate scattered across
> the land. What you see done in the halls of the politicians may
> not be wise, but it is the only real and viable definition of what
> the electorate wants.[3]

Though persuasive at first glance, it turns out that the economic-voter theory has a number of weaknesses. Eight points are worth examining in detail, not only because they call into question the theory, but also because they bear on other variants of the idea that the electoral process underlies the impulse to spend.

Economic self-interest voting in elections would rarely be rational, even for members of special interest groups. The economic-voter theory assumes that economically oriented behavior by the voter "pays off," that it makes sense for the voter to try and "buy" his government paycheck by voting for the politician who promises to approve his subsidy program.

What this logic overlooks is that a single vote represents an infinitesimal fraction of the governmental decision-making process. Consider the perspective of a single voter who stands to gain economically from a government subsidy program. Perhaps he is a farmer, or a food-stamp recipient. How should he behave to maximize his economic self-interest in an upcoming congressional election? The first thing this voter would notice is that his vote stands only an infinitesimal chance of changing the outcome of the congressional election. In these contests, well over 100,000 votes are cast, and the overwhelming majority are won or lost by 20,000 votes or more. The probability that this voter's single vote would decide the congressional election is too small to take seriously.

Furthermore, this voter would notice that even if his favored candidate won the election, he would be only one of 435 representatives and, hence, would have a correspondingly small chance of affecting the outcome of any given spending bill. Even if this congressman played the deciding role in the House of Representatives, there still is the Senate, and the presidency, and the bureaucracy. Any of these may veto, in one fashion or another, the spending desired by the voter. The higher spending might go through, for example, but along with it might come "tighter" regulations that could exclude this particular voter from the program altogether!

The connection between a single ballot and a favorable spending outcome is a chain of probabilities so tenuous that no thoughtful person would be tempted to depend on it. A rational voter single-mindedly pursuing his economic interest on election day would not waste his time voting. The people we see walking to the polls on election day are either not pursuing their economic self-interest, or they are not rational, or both.

It should be emphasized that we are speaking about *voting*. It probably *is* rational, at least in some cases, for economically motivated voters to *lobby* in favor of spending, to write their congressman, or to hire specialists to present their case in Washington. Lobbying is not voting, of course; it is a form of persuasion. As I point out at the end of this chapter, persuasion theory and electoral theories are often confused, with points that support the former mistakenly used in connection with the latter.

Voting on the basis of economic self-interest, if it occurred, might well pressure legislators to vote against, not for, spending. In its currently popular form, the economic-voting theory assumes that voters would never have any significant reason to oppose spending programs. But of course they would. They are taxpayers, and could save thousands of their own dollars if government spending were cut.

It is true that today, distortions and deceptions have grown up that obscure the full burden of government spending programs. These include everything from the way congressmen hide spending programs in late-night legislation, to deluding workers into assuming they are paying half as much social security tax as they are actually paying.[4] Taken together, these distortions are part of the prospending bias of the system, of course.

These biases are not logically implied by the pure economic self-interest theory of voting. They are, in fact, an outgrowth of the culture of spending, a result of broad prejudices and misunderstandings in favor of spending—such as the presumption of governmental efficacy and the inability of politicians to weigh opportunity costs (see Chapters 2 and 3).

In a purely economic theory of voting, there are no grounds for assuming that taxpayers will be misinformed and hoodwinked while the special interest beneficiaries will be well informed and efficient. We could just as easily assume that the taxpayers will be alert, knowledgeable, and irate about the effect of government spending on their pocketbooks. Under this assumption, they would, as voters, force politicians *not to spend*, leaving the country with an "underfinanced" public sector.

This variant of economic-voting theory is far from fanciful. It was, in fact, the view of a leading founder of the public-choice school of analysis, economist Anthony Downs. In his book, *An Economic Theory of Democracy*, Downs gave the theory of economic self-interest voting its first formal statement, a statement that still stands as the most comprehensive exposition of this idea.[5]

Today we are accustomed to hear, as something of a self-evident truth, that the operation of the electoral system underrepresents taxpayers and overrepresents special interests, and thus causes politicians to vote for excessive spending. The founder of economic-voting theory, however, was of precisely the opposite opinion. He wrote an entire article to "explain" theoretically "Why the Government Budget Is Too Small in a Democracy."[6] His idea was the one expressed above: Taxpayer-voters could see the money they were giving up in taxes, but they could not see the distant, indirect benefits of government spending programs. They would, then, prefer to keep their tax dollars—and would vote for politicians who agreed with them.

Since few today believe that the budget is "too small," the article mentioned has become something of an embarrassment to the economic-voting school of thought. I mention it not as an endorsement, but to illustrate the uncertain theoretical status of today's rational-voter theory that "predicts" big budgets. This is not a prediction that follows logically from the initial assumption that the voter is a selfish, "economic man." As the Downs article shows, this starting point can lead to almost any prediction you like, depending on the additional assumptions supplied.

In casting their ballot, voters may not be guided by economic self-interest. The economic-voting theory assumes that voters approach their choice by consulting their financial self-interest. It is not at all clear that voters can and do approach their task in this frame of mind. It is sometimes necessary to remind economists that human beings do many things without any thought or possibility of monetary consequences. For example, in professional baseball every year there is a balloting to decide on the composition of the all-star teams. Millions of people take the trouble to fill out ballots to decide who will win this "election." Are we going to say that these voters are motivated by financial self-interest? Surely the assumption is far-fetched.

From the voter's point of view, a congressional election may not be significantly different from a sports all-star election. Both are, simply, mass popularity contests. In both cases, the voter is making a shallow, superficial choice. In both cases he knows his choice won't make a significant difference. In both cases he is trying to pick people he likes or admires—or at least people whose names he recognizes. In both cases, it is doubtful that the voter sees in this decision an opportunity to affect his income.

Voters, including special interest voters, do not have the level of information necessary to connect their vote to a congressman's voting on spending. Over the past forty years, considerable research has been undertaken on the level of voter awareness about the political and policy world. These surveys have repeatedly found that voters are remarkably ignorant about even simple, dramatic features of the political landscape. The vast majority of voters cannot recall the names of congressional candidates in the most recent election; they cannot use the labels "liberal" and "conservative" meaningfully; they do not know which party controls Congress; they are wildly wrong about elementary facts about the federal budget, and they do not know how their congressmen vote on even quite salient policy questions.[7] In other words, they are generally incapable of rewarding or punishing their congressman for his action on spending bills.[8]

Voters tend to base their choices on superficial, nonpolicy voting cues. Although it may not square with democratic theory, the fact is that voting behavior is overwhelmingly shaped by factors other than the policy stands of candidates.[9] Voters pick one candidate over another mainly on the basis of three factors: party label, name recognition of the candidate, and the image of the candidate as honest, compassionate, friendly, unselfish, and intelligent.[10] Candidates win and lose elections mainly on the basis of advertising campaigns, not their votes on policy issues in Congress. A candidate's action on a spending measure would probably be, at best, only a minor factor in an election outcome.

These first several points can be illustrated by an examination of voter behavior in the one area where the economic-voting theory is thought to be most directly applicable: pork barrel projects. On local public works projects, it is thought, the selfishness of the voters comes most directly into play, so that congressmen are virtually forced to supply these visible, tangible benefits to win reelection. A typical expression of this view is given by J. Peter Grace, chairman of the President's Private Sector Survey on Cost Control:

> Spending is very important to congressmen. After all, the way congressmen get votes and guarantee loyalties back in the home district is by "bringing home the bacon," whether the projects thus supported are worthwhile or not. A fancy new highway here, a military base there, a new dam in the middle of nowhere—this is the stuff of long-term incumbency.[11]

This view of the electoral "power of pork" ignores all the points just raised. It assumes that voters vote their selfish economic interest; it assumes there is no economic self-interest in opposing a public works project; it assumes that voters know in advance who is to benefit from the project; it assumes that voters to be hurt by the project do not know in advance who they are; it assumes that voters will know how the congressman voted on the project; it assumes that they do not vote on the basis of other stimuli, especially the cues of party identification, name recognition, and image. Since each of these assumptions is to a degree untrue, the overall theory becomes quite tenuous.

Attempts to test the pork-barrel theory indicate little support for it. In one study, researchers measured the change in federal spending on construction in each district, and also the change in federal civilian employment, and tabulated these indicators of "pork" against the change in the congressman's electoral showing. They found no effect whatsoever:

> All in all, we found *no* evidence that obtaining local federal spending for his district or protecting against spending cutbacks is a useful way for a congressman to pursue reelection.[12]

Another way of testing the pork-barrel idea is to focus on cases when a congressman opposes a public works project *in his district*. Contrary to popular belief, congressmen do sometimes oppose these measures. In most such cases, the opposition is made rather undramatically: The congressman merely votes against a bill containing the project, or he fails to urge the inclusion of the project at some stage of the legislative process. Such relatively unpublicized opposition to a public works project would probably go unnoticed in the district back home, and for this reason would not afford a clear test of how voters react to such behavior.

There are a few recent cases, however, where the congressman's opposition to a project in his own district was visible and dramatic: He *led* a move to eliminate a project already approved. In each case, the congressman went on the record, literally, with an anti-project speech that appeared in the *Congressional Record*. An examination of four of these cases provides an extreme test of the electoral consequences of pork barrel voting. If there is anything to the popular view, all four congressmen should have been struck down by a lightning bolt of voter repudiation. In fact, all four did exceedingly well in the election that followed their presumed apostasy. Here are the cases:

- In 1983, Rep. Bob Wise (D–W.V.) urged the House to delete $26 million in funding for the proposed Stonewall Jackson dam in his district on the grounds that it was a wasteful approach to flood control. His move, incidentally, was opposed by West Virginia's other three congressmen.[13] In the 1982 election, Wise had obtained 58 percent of the two-party vote. In the 1984 election, after his move to eliminate the dam, he obtained 68 percent, an *increase* of ten percentage points.

- In 1984, Rep. Dan Lungren (R–Calif.) urged the House to eliminate a $20-million appropriation for the construction of a new federal building in his own district, arguing that in an era of deficits the project was expendable.[14] In the 1982 election, Lungren had obtained 71 percent of the vote; in 1984, after opposing the federal building, he was reelected with 75 percent, an *increase* of four percentage points.

- In 1986, Rep. Henry Waxman (D–Calif.) urged the House to strike funding for the Los Angeles Metrorail system on the grounds that it was not cost-effective and that it was dangerous to build. The initial segment of the system was 90 percent within his Los Angeles district.[15] In the 1984 election, Waxman had won with 63 percent of the vote. In the 1986 election, after going on record against the subway, Waxman ran unopposed and got 100 percent of the two-party vote.

- In 1975, Senator William Proxmire (D–Wis.) urged the Senate to terminate construction of a federally funded dam on the Kickapoo River in southwestern Wisconsin, on the grounds that it was expensive and environmentally unsound. The case was unusual in that Proxmire had been a supporter of the project, and the reversal of his position was probably more important in local reaction than the position itself. ("Lying Bill" Proxmire was hung in effigy by residents in La Farge, where the dam site was located, after his action). Proxmire also went to La Farge and held a meeting at which he defended his action to kill the dam to the stony faced and teary eyed townspeople.[16] Analysis of the election returns shows that Proxmire did suffer an electoral loss of 9.5 percent in Vernon county (where the dam was located) in following elections compared to his earlier showings. He still carried the county, but by 9.5 percent less than his projected strength.[17] Statewide, Proxmire did fine, with his vote increasing from 71 percent in 1970 to 73 percent in 1976.

These four cases indicate very little electoral risk in opposing local pork-barrel spending. In the three House cases, there appears to have been no negative electoral consequences of any kind following the member's dramatic opposition to a local public works project. In the Proxmire case, there was a negative effect locally, but this was practically stage-managed by Proxmire who took unusual steps to draw attention to himself as the nemesis of Vernon County. The local residents felt—perhaps not without reason—that Proxmire was making electoral hay at their expense.

It should also be noted that a number of congressmen have adopted a generalized "anti-pork" position in their campaigns, and they seem to do quite well electorally. In Missouri's Second District in 1986, for example, Republican candidate Jack Buechner ran against a leading long-time House pork-barreler, Democrat Robert Young, attacking Young for his "pork-barrel game of bringing home the bacon"—and won.[18] Democrat Bob Edgar of Pennsylvania led a twelve-year crusade against public works spending, and in the process held his seat in a strongly Republican district.[19] Texas Republican Dick Armey is an outstanding antispending congressman who has told his constituents that he "wasn't going to finish the day voting for pork for Texas."[20] Although voting against local projects, including a Job Corps center, he has increased his electoral margin.

Some spending programs do not have electorally relevant beneficiaries. Although most spending measures appear to have beneficiaries who, in theory, might punish a congressman for denying spending, a number of bills do not fall in this category. They are spending proposals with no identifiable beneficiaries, or at least no beneficiaries that might make an electoral difference to a congressman. They include spending programs for many traditional government activities, such as the FBI, the Customs Service, the Treasury, the State Department, foreign aid programs, the Library of Congress, and so on. The economic-voter theory cannot account for spending in these areas. Since voters have no direct financial stake in this spending, congressmen should be against it. Congressmen favor such "non-beneficiary" spending programs, however, just as much as spending that can be said to have beneficiaries.

Furthermore, the pattern of support for "nonbeneficiary" spending is the same as for all spending. To document this point, I selected three rather clear "nonbeneficiary" spending votes from the 1986 House session: The vote to authorize a higher level of aid to the Philippines (CQ 279), the vote to phase out the fourteen elevator operators who run elevators for congressmen (CQ 243), and the vote to create a $650,000 advisory commission to study intercollegiate athletics (CQ 347).

The Philippines vote did not involve beneficiaries who would vote in U.S. congressional elections; the fourteen elevator operators lived in the District of Columbia (and were not to be fired in any case); and the advisory commission was not yet in being—and in any case was too small to generate a significant number of economically affected beneficiaries. When the voting on these three measures is cross-tabulated with the general pattern of voting on all (nonmilitary) spending issues in Table 7.1, we see a strong congruence: Big spenders in general, when beneficiaries are involved, continue to be big spenders when no electorally relevant beneficiaries are involved.

The economic-voter theory will not readily account for this pattern. According to that theory, high-spending congressmen should be neutral toward spending that reaps no electoral reward.

TABLE 7.1   Support for Nonbeneficiary Spending Measures by High-,
Medium-, and Low-Spending Representatives, 1986

Spending category based on overall spending score[a]	Percentage voting for higher spending on:[b]		
	Philippines aid	Elevator operators	Athletic commission
High spenders	81	91	88
Medium spenders	35	45	51
Low spenders	14	9	11

a. The spending score is discussed in Chapter 5. It is based on a sample of thirty-six nonmilitary contested spending votes. The break points and Ns are as follows: high spenders, scores of 25–36, N = 212; medium spenders, scores of 10–24.5, N = 104; low spenders, scores of 0–9.5, N = 98. Total N = 414.
b. Absences are counted as higher spending votes.

The persuasion theory, on the other hand, will account for the pattern. It says that some congressmen are more persuadable than others. They more readily accept the philanthropic fallacy, which leads them to believe that government funds are "free," and that spending hurts no one. They are also more easily persuaded that government is efficacious in whatever it chooses to do. Therefore they will favor *any* spending that has a manifestly beneficent purpose. They are lulled into believing that a federal advisory commission will "help" whatever is wrong with intercollegiate athletics, or that U.S. government aid will "help" the Philippines. This same mentality carries over to spending measures that involve beneficiaries who happen to vote.

Congressmen are subjective in estimating voter policy preferences, tending to perceive these preferences in their own image. As we have seen, the economic-voting theory makes a number of unrealistic assumptions about voters. The problems with this theory do not end here, however; it also makes unrealistic assumptions about congressmen. For the theory to work, the congressman must make an accurate, objective assessment of the policy positions voters prefer. If—as theorized by the economic-voting theory—the congressman can gain votes by supporting spending, he needs to know it.

It turns out that this assumption of congressional awareness is unjustified: Congressmen generally do not make objective assessments about policy preferences of voters. Instead, they tend to project *their own* positions onto voters.

One certainly can't blame them for doing this, for the electorate itself does not speak intelligibly. The hundreds of thousands of people who make up a congressional district exhibit a wide diversity of opinions—as well as a considerable degree of apathy. As a result, the congressman can perceive the electorate as favoring almost any position he chooses to take.[21] Rather like the old-time theocratic rulers who saw the will of God to be whatever they wanted it to be, today's congressmen see the will of the people in the same subjective light. The district, or a majority of it, is perceived to favor whatever the congressman favors.

Even when objective data are available, it is not clear that congressmen and their staffs pay much attention to it. Few have the time or inclination to undertake statistical analyses of voting patterns to test hypotheses about what affected the outcome of an election. I asked two Proxmire aides about the electoral effect of the senator's stand on the Kickapoo dam, for example. One assumed, wrongly, that there had been no electoral effect in Vernon County; the other suspected a loss, but neither he nor anyone else in the senator's office had made the simple computations with electoral statistics to settle the issue.

On spending questions, it is possible for congressmen to conclude that the electorate is on whichever side of the issue they are on. The conservative Republicans who vote against most spending do not believe they are bucking their electorates; they assume that their district supports them. For example, conservative Republican Dick Armey—who had a score of zero on the 1986 House spending scale—believes his fiscal conservatism is popular with the voters. He argues that big-spending congressmen "underestimate the devotion of voters to the national interest, their willingness to sacrifice provincial interests for the national interest."[22] This is not to say that Armey is right or wrong; that would be difficult to assess. His case simply illustrates that congressmen can believe pretty much what they want to believe about the electorate.

A conservative Republican from the Northeast (with a 1986 spending score of 1) whom I interviewed observed that his successful predecessor in the same district for ten years had been a "moderate to liberal Democrat" on spending (which NTU spending ratings confirm). The congressman felt that this Democrat won elections because he was "personable" and "well-liked." Yet he supposed that the same constituents elected *him* for his antispending views:

R: I operate under the presumption that if I'm elected, each time, if I was elected in my last election, that the majority of people must have supported what I talked about. And what I talk about, for the most part, is that the number-one problem in America today is spending, or the budget deficit, and we're not dealing with that deficit.

It should be further pointed out that congressmen often feel, rightly or wrongly, that voters cannot or will not respond to certain types of spending issues. A moderate Democrat, for example, believed that the beneficiaries of the food-stamp program aren't electorally relevant. I had asked him whether there was an electoral impact from supporting or opposing the program (which he supported). He replied:

R: Food stamps is not an issue that will hurt me, because most people that benefit from food stamps generally don't participate in the political system. You've got a significant drop-off· in voting participation among the lower economic groups. And those single women with kids that are the biggest beneficiaries of food stamps generally don't vote, so there's not a lot of risk voting for or against the food-stamp program.

In conclusion, even if there were an objective "Thou must spend" message coming from the electorate, it is not clear that congressmen would hear it. Their subjective assumptions about what the voters want would get in the way.

The congressman's behavior on spending may have little to do with the goal of reelection. The economic-voting theory, painting congressmen from a very great distance, portrays them as machines that calculate the electoral advantage of each action and behave strictly according to the result of this calculation. This image involves a considerable distortion. On most policy choices, it is unclear to the congressmen how voting one way or the other will affect their electoral prospects. Therefore, they are relatively free to base their choices on the apparent merits of the programs.

Furthermore, many congressmen are not particularly worried about their electoral prospects. In some cases, the congressmen come from quite safe districts where they win both their primary and general elections handily, often without even facing an opponent. These legislators are not biting their nails about each legislative action, fearful that a "wrong" vote might result in an electoral defeat. Another group of congressmen are not concerned with electoral prospects because they are retiring from elective politics. Each year about a dozen House members voluntarily step down, announcing their decision early in their final year, if not before.

The behavior of these legislators is an important test of the electoral theory of spending. According to the theory, retirees would no longer be propelled by electoral necessity to approve spending. They can be "statesmen" and become fiscally more conservative.

Table 7.2 shows the 1986 spending scores for the twelve House members who retired at the end of the 1986 session, six Democrats and six Republicans. As the reader can see, these retirees are *not* more conservative, but slightly more in favor of spending than their fellow party members. When replicated using 1984 data, a different spending score and a different group of retirees, the same result occurs: The retirees are not more fiscally conservative.[23] This result confounds the expectation of the economic-voter theory. It is, however, consistent with the persuasion theory. Having been persuaded to favor a given level of spending, these retiring members simply go on voting for what they believe in. The reason they are slightly *more* in favor of spending than average is that, as a group, they are the more senior members who have been subjected longer to the persuasion of the culture of spending (see Chapter 5).

TABLE 7.2   Retiring Representatives' Spending

	Average spending scores	
	Democrats	Republicans
Representatives retiring at the end of 1986, not running for reelection	31.3	10.8
Representatives running for reelection or election to higher office, 1986	29.8	9.9

NOTE: The number of cases is Democrats retiring, 6; Republicans retiring, 6; Democrats not retiring, 236; Republicans not retiring, 166.

The Image-Protection Theory

The foregoing review indicates that the economic-voter theory of why congressmen prefer spending has a number of serious weaknesses. Many of the problems with this approach stem from its dependence on "economic-man" assumptions about voters and legislators, assumptions that are rather far from the reality of how voters and legislators behave. It seems that if these assumptions were relaxed, one could advance a somewhat more plausible theory.

Such a theory stresses "image protection." The key axiom in this theory is that congressmen are anxious to protect their image, that is, the public's distant, superficial perceptions about their basic virtues. Politicians want to appear kind, intelligent, honest, and hardworking; conversely, they do not want to appear cruel, stupid, dishonest, or lazy. Politicians want to protect their image partly because it helps them get elected, partly because it helps them get appointed to nonelected jobs (cabinet post, judge, or the like), and partly because it feels good to be approved of and not disgraced.

This focus on image is a realistic foundation for a theory about electoral processes because it takes into account voter behavior. As I noted, voters are generally not interested enough to know about and respond to a congressman's issue positions or legislative votes. They can, however, form a rough, distant impression about a candidate's virtues—just as they form similar impressions about baseball players or movie stars. The image-protection theory of spending says that special interest groups influence a congressman by threatening to harm his image if he votes against their desired spending.

An illustration might be spending for social security. If a congressman votes against this spending, this theory runs, the organizations of older Americans will "smear" the legislator as cruel and heartless. This negative image will affect some number of voters who will vote against the congressman in question. Many of these voters will be *younger* voters who will be economic losers if social security benefits are increased. In other words, in the image-protection theory, voters are not pursuing their selfish economic interests. They simply vote for nice-seeming candidates and against nasty-seeming ones. It is the pressure groups, working with and through the media, that manipulate the perceptions of nice and nasty.

One piece of evidence that suggests an image-protection effect comes from a study of election-year shifts in congressional voting. On rather visible, transfer-payment spending issues, there appears to be a tendency for congressmen who are electorally insecure to be more in favor of transfer payments in election years compared to nonelection years.[24]

There is considerable doubt, however, whether the image-protection idea will explain much of congressional spending behavior. Many of the objections to the economic-voter theory will also apply here.

Given the low level of voter awareness, most spending measures are too obscure to affect a candidate's image. A congressman votes on some two hundred spending measures each year. Only a handful of these could be made into an image campaign that might touch voters.

For most spending votes, there is great ambiguity about what the image effect might be. The congressman is therefore free to presume that the way he wants to vote is also the way to improve his image. To vote against agricultural subsidies, for example, might be made to seem cruel and heartless, but it can also seem to be a "courageous resistance to the powerful agribusiness lobby." Even voting against local public works projects can be thought to improve the congressman's image. An administrative assistant to anti-pork conservative Dick Armey believes that voters admire the congressman for his fiscal conservatism: "They say, 'Well, the guy obviously has principles.'"[25]

Senator William Proxmire is an example of a legislator who cultivated an antispending image, having made himself famous for opposing waste and giving out "Golden Fleece" awards for seemingly silly federal expenditures. He was reelected handily five times.

It is also important to remember that there are many different image cues in any election. A congressman's vote on a spending issue could be only one of dozens or even hundreds of other stimuli affecting voters. To a large extent, image cues are generated by the candidate and his organization in nonpolicy campaigning and self-advertising: newsletters, trips to the district, meetings with constituents, coffee hours, letters, help rendered to constituents, government pamphlets sent to constituents, handshaking, getting one's name in the papers, and so on. Congressmen see these nonpolicy self-promotion activities as vitally important to their election—and, the evidence suggests, correctly so.[26]

To take the Proxmire case as just one example, the senator's antispending stance was only one element in the electoral picture. He was also a tireless personal campaigner, returning to Wisconsin weekend after weekend to meet voters. As one of his aides put it, "80 or 90 percent of the people in his state feel that they know him." The same is true for most other congressmen: They are energetic personal campaigners who have built up personal followings. As a result, they can cast unpopular votes—on a spending issue, let us say—and still not see a significant electoral consequence.

A Direct Test of the Theories

In the preceding pages, we have looked at some variants of the idea that elections underlie the congressional impulse to spend. Our explorations indicate that the logic behind this notion is much weaker than commonly supposed. In the final analysis, however, the best way to evaluate a theory is not to criticize its assumptions but to test it. In the case of electoral theories of spending, this is rather easy to do.

Electoral theories of spending generally involve two main predictions. The first is that spending improves a congressman's electoral prospects. A direct test of this idea is to look at high and low spenders and see what happens to their electoral margins. If the electoral theories are correct, the high spenders should increase their electoral support, while those congressmen voting against spending should experience a decline.

The data for testing this idea for the House of Representatives are given in Table 7.3. Electoral changes are assessed by comparing a congressman's vote in 1984 with that of 1986. For example, if the congressman got 55 percent of the vote in 1984 and 60 percent in 1986, then his electoral margin increased 5 percent. In highly one-sided districts, large changes in electoral margins can be produced by the presence or absence of a major-party opponent; these misleading changes have been eliminated by confining attention to only those districts with regular two-party competition. Since there was a nationwide shift back to the Democratic party in 1986 (following the Reagan landslide of 1984), Democrats tended to improve more

TABLE 7.3   Does Voting for Spending Improve a Representative's
Electoral Margin? (1986)

Voting behavior during 1986[a]	Average increase in electoral margin, 1984 to 1986 (percentage)
Democrats:	
Medium spenders[b]	8.4
High spenders[c]	6.5
Republicans:	
Low spenders[d]	1.3
Medium spenders[e]	1.3

a. Based on only those congressmen who ran in the 1986 election, obtained less than 70 percent of the vote in 1984, and obtained less than 90 percent of the vote in 1986. Total N = 196.
b. 1986 spending score < 30; N = 37
c. 1986 spending score ≥ 30; N = 80
d. 1986 spending score < 12; N = 47
e. 1986 spending score ≥ 12; N = 32

than Republicans in the 1986 election. Therefore, the parties must be treated separately.

Since the parties occupy different ends of the spending scale, we have to divide our 1986 spending scale at different points to separate higher from lower spenders. For the Democrats, who have virtually no low spenders at all, we compare "medium spenders" with "high spenders." For the Republicans, who have few really high spenders, we compare "low spenders" with "medium spenders." As the reader can see, there is no sign that voters are punishing the lower spenders and rewarding bigger spenders. Among the Democrats, in fact, the big spenders do slightly *worse* than the medium spenders. Among Republicans, low spenders do just as well as medium spenders. For readers who appreciate the elegance of multiple regression analysis, this comprehensive test returns exactly the same conclusion as Table 7.3: *Voting more in favor of spending has no positive effect on a congressman's electoral margin.*[27]

It may be true that voting for spending doesn't help a congressman's election, but if congressmen did not know this, then there still could be an electoral effect. Electoral insecurity could drive congressmen to vote for spending. This is the second main prediction of electoral theories of spending. To test it, we need to see what effect electoral insecurity has on a congressman's disposition to vote for spending. The data for addressing this point are given in Table 7.4.

It is often forgotten that large numbers of congressmen are quite secure electorally. Their high name recognition ensures their victory in primary elections, and a favorable balance of party loyalties in their district ensures success in general elections. According to electoral theories of spending, these congressmen should be fiscal conservatives. Table 7.4 shows this expectation is confounded. The electorally secure congressmen are just as much in favor of spending as other congressmen.

Electoral theories of spending are also confounded by the behavior of the congressmen who are electorally insecure. According to the theory, they are supposed to be "running scared" and therefore voting for spending as a way to insure their survival. In fact, their behavior on spending issues appears unaffected by their precarious electoral situation. Again, multiple regression analysis, with controls for party and seniority, gives the same result.[28]

The conclusions are, then, that a congressman's support for spending does not seem to have any significant effect on his electoral showing, and a congressman's electoral insecurity does not seem to have any significant effect on his disposition to vote for spending.

We should keep in mind that these tests have used a representative sample of all contested spending issues as the basis of our

TABLE 7.4   Are Electorally Insecure Representatives More Likely to Vote for Spending?

Degree of electoral insecurity	Average spending score in 1986
Representatives who faced highly competitive contests in the 1984 elections[a]	20.4
Representatives who faced moderately competitive contests in the 1984 elections[b]	23.6
Representatives who faced no significant competition in the 1984 elections[c]	20.7

a. Representatives who won their 1984 primary election by a 10 percent plurality or less, or who won their 1984 general election by 55 percent or less; N = 71.
b. Representatives who won their 1984 primary election by an 11–40 percent plurality, or who won their 1984 general election by 56–65 percent; N = 134.
c. Representatives who won their 1984 primary election by at least a 41 percent plurality (or were nominated by convention) and who won their 1984 general election by at least 66 percent; N = 209.

spending score. On noncontested spending issues, where virtually all congressmen vote for spending, one might find a different result. The very fact that congressmen agreed suggests these might be issues—like Social Security or cancer research—where image protection is involved.

Cultural and Electoral Theories: The Overlap

We have seen that neither the logic nor the quantitative data offer much support for the usual electoral theories of spending. How, then, can we explain their great popularity?

The first answer is that electoral democracy is the creed of our civilization. The notion that citizens control public officials through the electoral process is an article of faith today, giving rise to the presumption that no matter what happens in politics, it is caused by elections. If the government budget seems "too low," then this is said to be the result of elections; if spending seems "out of control," then this, too, will be laid on the doorstep of democracy.

A second factor lending credibility to the electoral idea is the misinterpretation of legislative access. The public notices that lobbyists and pressure groups are extremely active in Washington, contacting congressmen and testifying in committees. The public also notices that congressmen often favor the spending programs urged by these lobbyists, spending programs that seem to be of doubtful merit. Observers thereupon conclude that the congressman has been "pressured" to vote for the "special interest" spending by the group's threat to vote against him unless he supports its spending program. In other words, legislative access is assumed to imply electoral pressure.

What this view overlooks is that access, the contact with the congressman, can be effective in quite a different way—through persuasion. When lobbyists meet with the congressman they are not threatening him with electoral defeat. They are giving him reasons for believing that the spending program is desirable. These "reasons" include both intellectual arguments about the policy as well as personal promptings that play on the congressman's desire to be a "nice guy." A veteran Washington observer describes this mechanism of social influence:

Why is access so vital? If the other side can't get similar access, a lobbyist's view may be all the official ever hears. [The] psychology of access plays on the fact that most government officials are basically decent people who want to be nice and want to be liked. Faced with a living, breathing fellow human being who wants something very much, with perhaps only an abstract argument on the other side, the natural reaction is to be obliging. That's why if you are a lobbyist, just getting through to a high official and presenting your case, using facts, figures, and persuasion—no favors involved—gives you a good chance for success. In fact, this is the way most lobbying victories are won.[29]

The interpretation of lobbying needs to be recast. Yes, lobbyists are highly visible in Washington, and, yes, they are influential in getting their special interest spending programs enacted. The mechanism of their influence, however, is not the threat of electoral retaliation. Were congressmen appointed to serve for life, with no need ever to run in elections, these lobbyists would probably be just as effective (assuming they met with congressmen as before). Their influence can be traced to their ability to persuade congressmen that each specific spending program is helpful. In the absence of anyone who says they are not, this is normally enough to win the day.

✦ 8 ✦

The Anomaly of Defense Spending

WE NOW TURN to the piece most difficult to fit into the puzzle: military spending. In this area, the usual expectations about spending are reversed, as if one had entered a world where up is down and down is up. This striking pattern constitutes both a challenge to, and an opportunity for, theories about spending. If they cannot accommodate the military spending exception, they fall under suspicion; if they can, they have passed an important test.

Two facts mark the exceptional character of military spending. The first is that in recent decades—that is, during the modern era of U.S.-Soviet hostility that began with the Korean War in 1950–1953—the relative size of U.S. military spending has been sharply declining. This comes as a surprise to many, since the public and the media tend to presume a pattern of alarming growth. Figure 8.1 shows the trend in the fraction of the gross national product devoted to defense. In broad terms, this has declined from around 10 percent in the late 1950s and early 1960s to around 6 percent today. The Reagan administration's military "buildup" did not restore prior levels of military effort, but only arrested the decline. Even before tensions with the Soviet Union eased in 1988–1989, defense spending had headed down again.[1]

Figure 8.1 reports the *relative* size of government spending, in comparison with the size of the economy. In direct contrast to the trend in military spending, domestic spending has increased

FIGURE 8.1   Federal Domestic and Military Spending as Percentage of GNP, 1955–1990

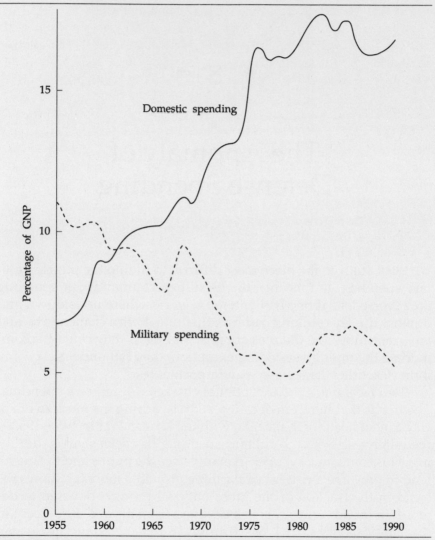

SOURCE: Office of Management and Budget, *Budget of the U.S. Government, Fiscal Year 1989* and *1991* (Washington, D.C.: Government Printing Office), table 6.1.

dramatically, from around 8 percent of the gross national product in the late 1950s to about 16 percent today.

The numbers show, then, that the spending problem that has overtaken us in recent decades has little to do with military spending. In fiscal and economic terms, military spending has gone *down*. The point can be illustrated by calculating what the federal budget would look like if domestic spending had matched the increase in military spending. Table 8.1 shows that if domestic spending had matched the trend in military spending since 1960, total 1989 spending would be over $435 billion lower than it actually was. Instead of a deficit of $152 billion, there would have been a surplus of $283 billion.

The American experience of soaring domestic spending and declining military spending is by no means unique. It reflects the pattern found in almost all the developed Western countries, from Austria to Canada, from Denmark to Mexico: In relative terms, domestic spending has been going up while military spending has been going down.[2]

The second anomaly about military spending concerns patterns of support. As shown in Chapter 6, there is a remarkable consistency in the support for domestic spending programs: Congressmen who vote for one type tend to vote for all the others. Congressmen who vote for welfare spending are also likely to vote for agricultural subsidies, for subsidies to big businesses, for subsidies to science, to education, to the arts, and even for programs that have no apparent beneficiaries. We saw that this consistent prospending orientation was characteristic of those congressmen generally called "liberals." Not to confuse them with their predecessors, I have called them "N-liberals."

TABLE 8.1   1989 Budget If Nondefense Spending Had Increased at the Same Rate as Defense Spending (billions of current dollars)

	1960 actual budget	1989 actual budget	1989 adjusted budget
Defense spending	48.1	303.6 (+531%)	303.6 (+531%)
Domestic spending	37.2	670.0 (+1,701%)	234.8 (+531%)
Interest payments	6.9	169.1	169.1
Total spending	92.2	1,142.7	707.5
Revenue	92.5	990.7	990.7
Surplus/deficit	+0.3	−152.0	+283.2

SOURCE: Office of Management and Budget, *Historical Tables: Budget of the U.S. Government, Fiscal Year 1989* (Washington, D.C.: Government Printing Office, 1988), tables 1.3 and 6.1; *Budget of the U.S. Government, Fiscal Year 1991* (Washington, D.C: Government Printing Office, 1990), tables 1.3 and 6.1.

When it comes to military spending, the pattern reverses. Those who support all types of general spending *oppose* military spending, and those who rather consistently oppose domestic spending *support* military spending. We can document this point with the military spending score developed in this study. This score is based on five military spending votes: three on specific weapons systems (the MX missile, the Bradley troop carrier, and the strategic defense initiative), a vote on withdrawing U.S. troops from Europe, and a vote on overall defense spending. They are combined into a single military spending score, which ranges from zero for a congressman who voted against the higher military spending alternative on all five issues, to 5.0 for a congressman who voted for higher spending each time (see the Appendix, "Measuring Congressional Spending," for details).

These military spending scores are cross-tabulated in Table 8.2 with the general spending scores based on the thirty-six votes for nonmilitary programs. The table shows a clear inverse relationship, with the high spenders on all types of domestic spending coming out with the lowest military spending scores. To some extent, the relationship follows party lines, with Democrats tending to be the high spenders who are antimilitary, and Republicans tending to oppose spending in general but supporting military spending. As the party breakdown in Table 8.2 shows, however, the relationship is

TABLE 8.2   Representatives' Support for Military Spending Compared to Support for Nonmilitary Spending, 1986

| Category on general spending[a] | Average military spending score (maximum possible score = 5) | | |
	All Representatives	Democrats	Republicans
High spenders[c]	1.6	1.6	3.0
Medium spenders[d]	3.8	3.1	4.1
Low spenders[e]	4.3	3.0[b]	4.4

a. The thirty-six-vote general spending score does not include any military-spending votes.
b. Only two cases.
The definition of each category and the Ns in the respective cells reading across is as follows:
c. Spending scores ≥ 25: N = 212, N = 202, N = 10
d. Spending scores ≥ 10, < 25: N = 104, N = 38, N = 66
e. Spending scores < 10: N = 98, N = 2, N = 96

not only, nor even mainly, a consequence of party membership. Within each party, the inverse pattern persists.[3]

It is significant to note that this pattern is rather recent. Back in the days of Eisenhower and Kennedy, defense spending was not a liberal-conservative issue. Democrats were as much in favor of military spending as were Republicans.[4] We have thus uncovered yet another issue on which modern liberals, whom we are calling N-liberals, differ from their predecessors.

The Theoretical Challenge

The military spending exception represents a serious obstacle for most theories of spending. These theories postulate mechanisms that should operate across the spectrum of spending programs. They predict, in other words, that all spending programs should grow. The experience in military spending—which has gone down relatively, and even, during the 1970s, absolutely—flatly contradicts this expectation.

Most of the formulations of the "public choice" school, for example, predict that any spending program, once established, will be maintained or increased. According to this theory, the beneficiary groups spawned by the program use their resources of votes or money to maintain or expand it.

One can hardly imagine a spending program more clearly destined for protection under this theory than defense spending. Consider the state of affairs in, say, 1962. There were 2,725,000 workers in defense industries—workers whose highly paid jobs depended on military spending. In addition, there were 2,808,000 military personnel and 1,240,000 civilian employees of the Department of Defense.[5] These "beneficiaries" of military spending were a nationwide force of aware and relatively alert voters. In addition to the workers, there were the officers, stockholders, lawyers, lobbyists, and PR specialists of the defense industry corporations—General Dynamics, Boeing, Lockheed, and so forth. Furthermore—this theory would continue—the military spending lobby had the best of all "smokescreens" to hide behind: It spoke for "national defense," "patriotism" and "anti-communism." All in all, this military spending lobby would represent the most awesome special interest group to which Congress had ever been subjected. Alongside it, the usual lobbies of dairy farmers,

Navajo Indians, or rural telephone subscribers would be little more than gnats.

What was the effect of this lobby of lobbies on spending? Military spending fell dramatically from the early 1960s to the late 1970s, and military jobs and contracts shrank proportionally. In fact, *about one million defense industry jobs were lost over this period.* This outcome throws considerable doubt on the idea that the spending process is controlled by selfish, "rent-seeking" interests who coerce congressmen into supporting programs of benefit to them.

Another theory called into question by the defense spending experience is the "logrolling" idea. In broad terms, this theory says that congressmen form a trading network among themselves whereby each votes for spending measures favored by the others in order to receive support for their own preferred spending measures. Congressmen are motivated to participate in this process by their need to feel important and demonstrate their "power," and by their desire for approval by their peers.

In this theory, spending programs become "chips" in a rather private game of influence and prestige played in Washington, a game that has little to do with the voters or with actual national problems. Congressmen become identified with programs— sometimes almost by accident—and therefore their prestige is affected. If the program is cut, they come out looking like "losers," but if it is expanded, they are "winners." Congressmen quickly realize that they cannot be winners all by themselves: They need the support of other players. To get that support, they have to vote for the spending programs of their colleagues. Once this whole system gets going, it drives spending for all programs higher and higher.

This theory may occasionally apply to some spending programs, but it does not seem to be a major explanation for why congressmen support spending programs. The defense spending exception we are examining is one important piece of evidence against it. If logrolling drives spending, then it should have driven military spending, too. Surely there were congressmen identified with various arms programs and with various defense plants and military installations in their districts who stood to come out looking like losers if defense spending were cut. They would have used a logrolling system to maintain and increase military spending.

The pattern of voting is further evidence against the logrolling idea. If there is a variation among congressmen in the degree to which they participate in the logrolling game, these variations should be consistent across all issue areas. If congressmen play this game for reasons having nothing to do with the apparent merits of the programs themselves, then big logrollers on issue A should also be big logrollers on issue B, and so on. Those who don't play the game—either because they think it is immoral, or because they are less concerned with personal status seeking—should not play any part of it. As I documented above, this consistency does not occur. Congressmen who vote for spending in general vote *against* military spending, and congressmen who vote against the general array of domestic programs are the ones voting *for* military spending.

In conclusion, the facts about military spending are rather hard on many of the popular theories of spending. These theories are at odds with the salient features of this spending: In relative terms, military spending has been trending downward, contradicting the upward trend of domestic spending; and the politicians who support domestic spending tend to be opponents of military spending, and supporters of military spending tend to be opponents of general domestic spending.

Military Spending and Persuasion Theory

The thesis of this book is that the behavior of congressmen on spending programs is a function of their perception of the merits of these programs. When they vote for a spending program, they do so because they believe that it is a helpful or responsible way of addressing a particular problem. In other words, their vote reflects what they have been persuaded to believe about the program.

Most other theories of spending ignore or deny this point of view. The congressman's decision on a spending measure is presumed to come from some personal motive, such as his desire to be reelected, or his desire for fame, or his desire for personal wealth. The apparent merits of the programs do not play a role. The pros and cons about the program are said to be post hoc rationalizations: The congressman first decides to back a spending measure based on some selfish motive, and then points to lofty arguments about human betterment to justify his position.

In previous chapters, we have explored the weaknesses of this cynical perspective, weaknesses that are both logical and empirical.

The military spending issue constitutes another point on which self-interest theories of congressional behavior falter. It does not seem that one can explain this pattern without taking into account how congressmen perceive the rights and wrongs of the issue itself. In broad terms, I am suggesting that military spending has gone down because a majority of congressmen have come to feel that *this* spending is unnecessary or harmful. There has been a change in perspectives on military spending, a change in what congressmen believe.

An explanation of the decline in military spending, therefore, must look to the factors that affect how congressmen go about making up their minds on spending issues. In this book, I have focused attention on two aspects of the belief-formation process: how congressmen weigh the manifest and latent aspects of policy issues, and how congressmen are persuaded through personal contacts with administrators, lobbyists, and constituents.

Both these aspects are important in shaping congressional views on military spending, but the first is clearly the most important. In Chapter 6, to explain the difference between the parties on domestic spending issues, I introduced the idea that on many policy questions there were competing "manifest" and "latent" arguments. The manifest feature of a policy is its apparent, direct consequence; latent features involve the indirect or hidden consequences. In a program intended to provide housing for the homeless, for example, the manifest aspect is the appealing aim of helping unfortunate people. The latent aspects include the harm to the unseen individuals taxed to pay for the program, as well as theories that suggest the program will fail, make the problem worse, or cause other problems. I suggested that politicians vary in the degree to which they respond to manifest as opposed to latent aspects of policy issues. The N-liberals, who are mostly Democrats, are the ones who tend to emphasize manifest features in their thinking. The N-conservatives, who are mainly Republicans, are more affected by latent considerations.

On most budget issues, those emphasizing the manifest perspective would lean toward more spending because spending seems an immediate, direct way to address the problem—as in the illustration of spending for the homeless. Those politicians who emphasize the latent aspects of spending—the hidden and long-run costs—would be inclined to oppose the typical spending measure. This reasoning accounts for why N-liberals support so many different kinds of spending programs, and why N-conservatives oppose these programs (or favor lower levels of spending for them).

This formulation assumes, of course, that the manifest aspect of the spending program is attractive. It assumes that in an immediate sense, the spending is directed toward a positive or helpful end. If this were not true, when the spending seems directed toward some harmful purpose, then the theory predicts that N-liberals should vote *against* it. If, at the same time, there were latent implications of the spending that were beneficial, then N-conservatives would vote *for* it.

Military spending in normal times is this kind of issue. In immediate terms, one seems to be purchasing the means for killing and destroying. As former Rep. James Weaver (D–Ore., 1984 ADA rating of 100) put it, military spending is buying "weapons of holocaust."[6] N-liberals, reacting in terms of manifest appearances, are thus prompted to vote against repugnant military spending.

The arguments *for* military spending in peacetime are latent; that is, they rely on indirect, hidden connections. Perhaps the most common argument is that one deters possible aggressors from initiating a campaign of conquest by threatening them with defeat and destruction if they do so. If this theory is correct—and notice that it is a theory—then one maintains peace by acquiring the repugnant "weapons of holocaust." Legislators disposed to weigh latent considerations—the N-conservatives—are therefore more likely to support military spending.

In this theory, the opposition of N-liberals to military spending does not reflect a comprehensive antimilitary philosophy. When military spending seems needful in an immediate sense—as it would when the country was attacked, or when a war seemed moral—then N-liberals will support it.[7] N-liberals will also support aspects of military spending that have an appealing or helpful appearance, such as higher wages for personnel or higher benefits for veterans.

This theory of manifest and latent perspectives will account for the inverse pattern of support for military and nonmilitary spending. It can be extended, in principle, to account for the patterns of behavior on any kind of spending: N-liberals will follow the manifest aspect and N-conservatives will be affected by latent aspects. This principle explains why N-liberals favor (nonmilitary) foreign aid (even though it is not popular with voters). In manifest terms, foreign aid seems well-intentioned and helpful in the same way domestic spending programs will seem, at first glance, helpful.

Within this theory, how do we account for the decline in military spending? The main answer is that the military spending issue has changed its appearance. In the 1950s, the threat posed by the Soviet Union was dramatic: A satellite empire had just been created, China had fallen to communism, Berlin had been blockaded, South Korea had been invaded. In effect, the wartime perspective on military spending dominated. The manifest aspect of military spending in those days, then, was the need to counter the imminent danger to ourselves and our allies. More recently, the perception of danger from the Soviet Union and communism has declined greatly, so that the manifest aspect of the issue is the ugliness of war and preparations for war.

Persuasion and Military Spending

In the main, congressional positions on military spending seem to be determined by the manifest/latent perspectives just discussed. There is more to the picture, however. There is a process of persuasion taking place in the immediate congressional environment, and this persuasion appears to have an additional effect on congressional views.

For military spending, these effects are more complex than on other spending issues. On the normal spending issue, the system produces consistent, prospending stimuli on all levels. The informal contacts with constituents and group representatives will favor spending, the media will have the same slant, and so will the official sources of information and opinion: documents, reports, program administrators, testimony at hearings.

On the military spending issue, the general, informal communications tend to be quite mixed, producing, in many instances, antispending stimuli. The underlying reason for this pattern is, simply, that ours is an antimilitary culture. The point is not sufficiently appreciated, but the evidence for it—which I have presented elsewhere—is considerable.[8] Historically, for example, the United States (along with Great Britain) led the world in size of its antiwar religious congregations, including explicitly antiwar groups like Quakers and Mennonites, as well as major denominations with a strong antiwar bias, including the Methodists, Congregationalists, and Presbyterians. Peace societies, which grew up in the nineteenth century, flourished only in the United States and Britain: The first in the world was the New York Peace Society, founded in 1815.

For most of its history, the United States has had a minuscule standing army and established a clear pattern of being militarily unprepared for the conflicts it entered, including even the campaigns against the Indians. Even today, despite many foreign challenges and involvements, the United States is below the world average in the level of effort it makes to field a military establishment.[9] Opinion polls typically find that more Americans favor cutting military spending than support increasing it; in 1987, over three times as many people felt military spending was "too much" (44 percent) as thought it "too little" (14 percent).[10] Exaggerating what they consider "evil," Americans consistently overestimate the size of the military budget.[11] Antimilitary and disarmament organizations are surprisingly numerous. One directory of peace organizations for the seven mid-Atlantic states identifies 966 such groups.[12] A compilation of disarmament groups in northern and central California contains over 625 listings.[13] A tabulation of peace and disarmament groups nationwide lists some 5,700 organizations, including over 400 national-level groups.[14]

The media tends to associate itself with the antimilitary position. Whereas the bias on domestic spending runs in favor of spending (as discussed in Chapter 4), on military spending the media favors the antispending side.[15] The antimilitary groups and antimilitary sentiment in U.S. society means that many congressmen receive communications against military spending. A number of congressmen and staff mentioned in interviews that they receive letters and constituent comments against military spending, both in general and concerning specific programs. At the informal level, then, congressmen are the recipients of considerable antimilitary persuasion.

In the more formal policy-making and committee-hearing process, however, the stimuli clearly favor spending. The overwhelming majority of witnesses at committee hearings and policy briefings are administrators and officers from the Department of Defense who make the case for spending. The nongovernment witnesses mainly support defense programs, too. They include representatives from defense contractors, from organizations of defense contractors, from military technology organizations, and from prodefense lobbies.

Although, as noted above, there are thousands of antimilitary organizations in the country, they rarely appear in these meetings, perhaps deterred by the possibility of a hostile reception.

The overall picture, then, seems to be that the average congressman probably receives neutral or somewhat antimilitary communications, whereas those congressmen serving on committees supervising military programs are more exposed to the promilitary point of view. One test of this idea is to compare the military spending scores of such congressmen with those of their peers (Table 8.3). The results support the theory: Members of the Armed Services Committee and the Military Subcommittee of the Appropriations Committee are more in favor of military spending than is the average member of the House.[16]

How to Cut Spending

Because it constitutes an exceptional case of spending decline, military spending gives us a broad overview of what is necessary to bring about a major reversal in spending trends in other areas. Military spending has declined because, in terms of immediate perceptions, it now seems a distasteful, unappealing type of spending.

To bring about major cutbacks in other types of spending programs, this experience suggests, a massive realignment in percep-

TABLE 8.3   The Effect of Military Oversight Committee Membership on Representatives' Military Spending, 1986

	Average military spending score	
	Democrats	Republicans
Members of House Armed Services Committee[a]	3.1	4.7
Members of House Military Appropriations subcommittee[b]	3.8	4.8
Other representatives (not members of above committees)[c]	1.6	4.1

The number of cases in each subgroup is:
a. N = 27, N = 16
b. N = 6, N = 4
c. N = 209, N = 152

tions must take place. The persuasion on the spending issue must be so broad and effective that the manifest aspect of the program becomes negative. It is not enough to show by theoretical arguments that this or that spending program is unsound. These arguments do not reach the majority of politicians, who are responsive to issues in terms of their simple, manifest features. To affect them, the case against spending needs to be made with tactics that communicate the harm of spending in a graphic, self-evident way.

III

Controlling Spending

✦ 9 ✦

Legal Spending Limits

THE GROWING CONCERN about government spending has fostered a parallel growth in proposals for doing something about it. New organizations have been formed, politicians and activists have agitated for reforms, symposia and conferences have considered alternatives and made recommendations.

Where are these proposed solutions taking us? Are they likely to succeed in the long run? To discuss these questions, it is helpful to group the proposals under main headings that cover their essential characteristics. In analytic terms, there appear to be three main approaches to limiting government spending:

- Adopting legal devices that attempt to limit spending
- Countering the culture of spending by persuasion directed against specific spending programs
- Countering the culture of spending by controlling indoctrination effects, especially by limiting congressional terms

In this chapter, I shall examine the legal approach; the following chapters will examine the other two methods.

The Legalism Illusion

My first encounter with legal devices for limiting government spending came some twenty-five years ago when I was studying the legislature of Colombia for my doctoral dissertation. In this South American country, mismanagement of fiscal policy was the order of the day, with budgeted expenditures rather consistently exceeding revenues. Sometimes the government couldn't pay its debts, and simply left schoolteachers or postal employees without their paychecks. Much of the time the national treasury was resupplied by expanding the money supply, with the result that the country suffered inflation, high interest rates, and a constantly deteriorating international exchange rate.

Aware of this background, I was reading the Colombian constitution one day when my eye fell on Article 211. Lo and behold, the Colombian constitution contained a balanced budget provision! "Neither Congress nor the executive may propose an increase or new expenditure in the budget," it declared, "if the increase alters the balance of budgeted expenditures and budgeted revenues."[1] What surprised me was not just the fact that the clause was obviously not working, but that no one in Colombian politics gave it any notice. I had interviewed many deputies and senators, and none had mentioned it.

The next day, I went to a deputy on the appropriations committee and asked him about this clause. "Oh, that," he said with a deprecating wave of his hand. "It has no effect, because whenever they want to propose an increased expenditure, they just increase the amount of the expected revenue by the same amount. So the budget still *looks* balanced." As I inquired further, I found there was more than just cynical arithmetic to the ineffectiveness of Article 211. The government revenues were constantly shifting, with new taxes and different tax schedules being applied. In this ambiguity, even well-intentioned budgetmakers would have difficulty naming a "true" revenue figure. Furthermore, much of Colombian budgeting was done through the use of "emergency" appropriations not covered by the article.

It was a good lesson for a student of politics, a dramatic reminder of the elementary proposition that *laws are not self-executing.* We all know this, of course. We know that a law against littering doesn't stop littering, that a law against speeding doesn't stop speeding. Nonetheless we are attracted by the "legalism illusion," the belief that by putting our aims down on paper, and having the document approved by a suitably august body, we have solved the problem that vexed us. In this view, government is like a railroad engine. The formal documents—constitution, organization charts, legal codes—are the tracks that determine where the engine must go, regardless of what the politicians in charge may desire. If you change what the documents say, then by this theory you have necessarily changed the direction of policy.

When it comes to limiting spending, the legalism illusion leads us astray even more than usual, for this is an area where laws alone would be particularly unlikely to be effective. First, fiscal policy is fraught with complexities and ambiguities. The idea of limiting spending seems simple, but the actual activities whereby spending takes place are highly complex, involving complicated budget and revenue proposals, decisions made by dozens of different bodies at different times, and actions by thousands of administrators. In all this extensive, collective activity, it is extremely difficult to point to specific deeds that constitute the spending "crimes" and the specific individuals who "committed" them.

Second, limiting spending is a political question. We cannot depend on the FBI or the Capitol Police to see that the provisions against spending are enforced. It falls to the politicians themselves to enforce them. For all practical purposes, they become prosecutor, judge, and jury in deciding who has "violated" an antispending provision and in determining what the punishment or corrective action shall be. Since these same politicians have approved the spending in the first place, it is unreasonable to expect them to punish themselves for wrongdoing—especially when, as I just noted, the crime itself is so ambiguous.

We reach the conclusion, then, that a legal provision to limit spending cannot by itself have an effect. If the politicians themselves approve of spending, then an antispending law will be evaded, reinterpreted, or ignored.

We do not need to go all the way to South America to demonstrate the point. The United States has had its share of laws and procedures designed to check spending but which have not, in fact, operated to check spending.[2] One of the most dramatic failures in this regard is the 1974 Congressional Budget and Impoundment Control Act.

By the early 1970s, it was becoming clear that the federal budget was out of control. Spending was marching upward at a seemingly inexorable rate; nine of the past ten years had seen deficits; inflation had become an alarming problem. To address this problem, Congress created a system that was supposed to provide for orderly budget making and a balanced budget. Budget committees were established and were given the mission of proposing overall budget targets that would keep spending within expected revenues. These budget committees were given extensive staff to make all the relevant computations, and a new congressional agency was established, the Congressional Budget Office, to supply data and make projections. On paper, it looked like a rational, responsible system for controlling spending. In signing the bill into law, then–President Nixon pointed out that the previous budget system

> [did] not impose sufficient disciplines on the Congress to stop the passage of pork-barrel legislation or to resist the pressure of special interest groups. . . . This lack of discipline in Congressional procedures has been one of the major factors behind the sizable increases in Federal spending over the past decade.
>
> The Congress has wisely recognized these weaknesses and taken steps to correct them through the passage of this legislation.[3]

In practice, the 1974 budget act was a dismal failure. After it was put into effect, the federal budget continued to grow, showing a deficit in every single year, and each deficit larger than any of the deficits in the years before the act was adopted. The provisions of the act were simply evaded or overruled by the Congress itself. By adopting generous spending "targets"—and by waiving those targets time and again—congressmen went ahead and spent what they wanted to spend.[4]

The Gramm-Rudman-Hollings Act

In 1980, the mood in the United States swung against government spending. Years of deficits and years of increasing taxation jelled into a diffuse perception that spending was "bad," that it was a "problem" decision makers needed to address. The changing public attitude toward spending was not the result of any particular tactic or campaign. In many ways, it was like the sentiment of war weariness that will overtake a people after many years of fighting. After years of spending growth, inflation, and high interest rates, a reaction had set in, a reaction that affected all politicians, liberals and conservatives.

This sentiment focused on spending *in general*. The government's fiscal problems and wrongdoings were perceived in terms of the total amount being spent. This concern grew partly out of the traditional American aversion to "big government" and the realization that a big budget *was* big government. Even more important in focusing attention on spending was concern about the deficit. For reasons not entirely clear, after 1980 the public, pundits, and politicians came to consider the federal deficit alarming, an evil on which all other economic problems, from unemployment to high interest rates, were blamed. It is mainly for its role in causing the deficit that spending—total spending—has been condemned.

Most of the antispending forces took up this opposition to spending and sought legal ways to make it effective. One of the leaders of a Washington antispending group explained the thinking behind this approach:

Q: What's your main approach to the spending issue?

R: There probably is a main theme, and that is to aggregate the issues. Politically, people are much more against the overall level of spending than they are against a particular program. Every particular program always has some interest group that's giving very persuasive, albeit unjustified, cases for why the program should exist and why you shouldn't cut their funding—you know, "you'll have people dying in the snow in the cold."

So we want to look at the overall level of spending, and issues that spring from that, such as a spending freeze, and a balanced budget amendment. Those are the types of things that we're much more able to build political support around.

The centerpiece of the 1980s campaign to control spending in general was the Gramm-Rudman-Hollings budget measure. This act, signed into law by President Reagan on December 12, 1985, provided for a mandatory process to bring about the reduction and elimination of the budget deficit. Its basic provision was a requirement that the budget deficit should be reduced year by year and eliminated by 1991. If Congress failed to pass budgets that limited spending, then cuts were to be applied automatically, bringing the deficit down to the required level.

Although adopted with high hopes, the Gramm-Rudman law was no more successful in limiting spending than the earlier 1974 budget act. Somehow, in all the confusion of budget conferences, broken spending-reduction pledges, and biased budget estimates, the law was never adhered to. The original law called for the deficit to be reduced to $36 billion in 1990 and eliminated in 1991.[5] As the years passed, these targets receded. The actual budget for 1990 had a deficit of $220 billion, over six times what had been mandated. For 1991, the budget targets were all but thrown away to allow for an expected $254 billion deficit.

Just like the Colombian politicians, U.S. budget writers engaged in deceptive "gimmicks" to meet the letter of the law while not actually limiting spending. The savings and loan bailout costs, for example, have been placed off-budget, paydays of government employees have been shifted to understate current spending, and government office space has been acquired through lease-purchase arrangements that shift costs into the future.[6] Thus one result of the Gramm-Rudman law has been to make federal budget figures distorted and undependable.

The *coup de grâce* for Gramm-Rudman came in October 1990. Faced with a projected 1991 budget deficit vastly higher than even the amended deficit targets, President Bush and congressional leaders worked out a new budget law that effectively ended legal budgetary restraints. This new budget agreement shocked observers who had looked to the budget-negotiating process for spending "cuts." Instead, the new agreement provided for at least $245 billion in domestic spending increases over its five-year life.[7] The 1991 spending level for housing subsidies, for example, was increased 22 percent over 1990; National Science Foundation spending grew by 13 percent; National Aeronautics and Space Administration spending was increased by 13 percent; new-construction spending for the Park Service and Fish and Wildlife Service was increased 43 percent; the appropriation for the Departments of Labor, Education, and Health and Human Services included a 13-percent yearly increase for new initiatives, and so on.[8]

To fund this increased spending, negotiators adopted tax increases of $137.2 billion—a move which meant that President Bush abandoned, in humiliation, his campaign pledge not to increase taxes. A second "source" of the increased spending would be an increased deficit: The budget agreement projected this to increase to a record $254 billion in 1991.

The October 1990 budget agreement showed what the relative priorities in Washington are. When the chips are down, Congressional majorities believe that expanding government programs is more important than holding the line on taxes, more important than reducing the deficit, and certainly more important than legal spending restraints. These priorities mean that the outlook for any legal remedy to the spending problem, even a constitutional amendment to limit spending or balance the budget, is unpromising. Even if adopted, it is improbable that such legal devices would function effectively.

The Anatomy of "Hypocrisy"

The repeated failure of the legal efforts to restrain spending raises an interesting question: Why are legal spending limits adopted? If congressmen—and presidents—don't believe in limits, why do they go through the bruising and humiliating exercise of adopting them and then repudiating them? The popular explanation is that congressmen are being hypocritical. They adopt the spending limits to "look good," knowing full well that they disagree with them and intend to subvert them later.

The problem with this theory is that congressmen certainly don't "look good" when they are in the act of overturning the spending limits. Those who pay attention to the budget process will know who supported a spending limit and who betrayed that limit later. President Bush's 1990 reversal on his "no new taxes" election campaign pledge is a case in point: His public opinion rating dropped some twenty points. Flip-flopping on budgetary issues is not the road to high public esteem.

In order to understand the reversals and inconsistencies on fiscal policy, we have to begin with an accurate assessment of the intellectual calibre of congressmen. Washington politicians are not ten feet tall, capable of looking thoughtfully into the future to discern the effect of measures on either the country or on their own image. They can be shallow and shortsighted like anyone else, responding to the stimuli and impressions of the immediate context. With this fact in mind, it is easy to understand why they adopt and

then overturn spending limits. The process involves a simple conflict between general and specific stimuli.

The overall point is obvious: Unrestrained spending is the road
to economic disaster. Somehow, somewhere, a line against more
spending must be drawn. Even a child can see this, and most
congressmen grasp it, too. Therefore, when a legal spending limit is
proposed, the first impulse of most congressmen, even big spenders, is to go along with the idea.

Unfortunately, this general truth comes into conflict with all the
specific spending programs in the budget. As we have seen,
congressmen are exposed to an indoctrination in favor of each program, and they respond positively to this persuasion. They come to
believe that each program is a needed response to a serious national
problem. The result is inconsistency: Congressmen wind up being
in favor of both spending limits and more spending.

When the inconsistency has to be resolved in the final budget
package, it is not surprising to find that politicians favor protecting
the specific programs. The harm of cutting specific programs will
seem quite definite and concrete, but the harm of letting spending
rise a little more will seem diffuse and far away.

This is how "hypocrisy" on the spending question is generated.
Policy makers start out criticizing a "bloated budget," but at close
range they find that this budget consists of many specific programs,
each of which is supported by an entire symphony of arguments, biased studies, pseudostatistics, and socially approved assumptions.
Furthermore, as I have made clear, this harmony is rarely disturbed by
discordant notes from opponents of specific programs. Supporters of
programs overwhelm the councils of government. When the policy
makers look more closely at what government is doing in agriculture,
let us say, they discover a food-stamp program that is said to keep 20
million Americans from starving, or a soil-conservation program without which the entire United States would wash into the Gulf of Mexico.

When the innocent enters policy realms armed only with the
general idea that "spending is bad," he is easily seduced, for this
abstract homily is overpowered by visions of starving millions and
eroding continents. The situation is not unlike sending a farm boy to
town and telling him to "keep out of trouble." Because he is unaware of all the appealing and subtle forms "trouble" can take in
specific instances, this general advice is practically worthless.

The evolution of the Reagan administration clearly illustrates how a general orientation against spending is undermined by the appeals of specific programs. Budget Director David Stockman was given the job of making cuts in the budget, but little attention was given to making the case about what was wrong with the programs to be cut. Stockman reports that even President Reagan was uninformed about the specific content of his budget-cutting program. "When he was later called on to justify the cuts, he would remember only that he was making the cut, not why."[9]

The result was that Reagan's 1981 budget-reduction package gradually came apart. When they looked at the proposed cuts, administration officials discovered that program after program had a seemingly persuasive rationale. In many cases, they were swayed by these justifications and joined the ranks of the big spenders. The administration's support for the "safety net" of big-budget social spending was one betrayal of the antispending cause, but only one. On many programs, from federal science subsidies to energy projects, the administration led the way to higher spending.

The fate of the Department of Education illustrates the pattern. Created by the Carter administration, this department was criticized outside Washington as an unnecessary expansion of the federal role. The Republican platform of 1980 pledged to abolish it, and candidate Reagan endorsed that pledge. Year by year the promise was forgotten as education officials kept arguing in favor of this spending, while no one took up the job of making the specific case against it. The result was not a department eliminated, but one whose budget grew from $15 billion in 1980 to $22 billion in 1989.

Even when the Reagan administration opposed programs, its opposition was so shallow that it wound up supporting them. For example, the Reagan administration made a genuine effort to cut back numerous programs in agriculture, submitting reduced budgets to Congress. In "defending" these reductions, however, the administration lauded the programs involved! In introducing its 1989 budget for the system of crop subsidies and credits, for example, the administration budget message declared: "Federal agricultural programs help meet domestic and international trade demands for food and fiber while mitigating the adverse effects of price fluctuations on farmers."[10] The logical implication of this endorsement of agricultural subsidies is that the programs should be maintained, or even expanded. If the federal programs are so useful, the observer has to wonder, shouldn't they be strengthened?

When the Reagan administration would be "accused" of cutting a program, it did not proudly take credit for (trying to make) cuts. Instead, it squirmed in embarrassment, confirming its opponents' premise that cutting programs was wrong. For example, when Senator Edward Kennedy and other liberals accused the administration of "unconscionable budget cuts" in federal food assistance programs in 1988, the administration ran for cover. The administrator of the Food and Nutrition Service dispatched a letter to the *New York Times* to rebut the charge: "Readers should know that our annual $20.5 billion food assistance budget is the highest ever, $6.2 billion higher than in 1980."[11] Thus she reinforced the view that spending on food programs was "nice," something that all well-intentioned people agree should be increased.

When *Time* alleged that the Reagan administration "made student loans harder to get," Vice President Bush refuted the claim by declaring that "federal aid to college students has increased by 75 percent since we took office."[12] When the same magazine claimed that "subsidized housing has been slashed 77 percent," Reagan's Secretary of Housing and Urban Development said, "Wrong; it has been doubled. The actual amount paid by the federal government has increased from $5.3 billion in 1980 to $12.3 billion in 1988."[13] These cases illustrate the media perspective on spending examined in Chapter 4, the view that spending programs solve problems and that spenders therefore wear the white hats. What is remarkable is the adoption of the same perspective by fiscal conservatives.

In this fashion, the Reagan administration wound up strengthening the case for spending in just about every area. Instead of arguing that the program in question was wasteful and harmful, it agreed with its critics that each program was worthy and that boosting spending for it was something to be proud of. The "Reagan revolution" was of uncertain value in the effort to control spending. Some spending restraint did occur as this administration implemented the diffuse public mood against spending. Intellectually, however, the administration gave considerable reinforcement to the attitude that government spending programs represent a healthy approach to our problems.

The Reagan administration is not the only example of how a shallow "spending-is-bad" focus leads to inconsistency. Other antispending campaigns have the same problem. The theme of eliminating "waste," which a number of antispending groups have taken up, illustrates the issue. If one starts out seeking to control spending in general, then *any* government dollar saved is a plus. One way to save the government money is to find ways to make programs more efficient, to get the same job done for less money. One might point out, for example, that by using a soy flour extender in hamburgers, the school-lunch program can save a million dollars. Once this efficiency is adopted, a million dollars of taxpayer money has been saved. In the short run, spending will be lower. Unfortunately, the overall effect of this activity is to *strengthen* support for government spending on the school-lunch program. In urging that the school-lunch program should be more efficient, the speaker is reinforcing the premise that there *should be* a federal school-lunch program, that the program is needed and necessary. In making the program more efficient, he is making it more attractive. Furthermore, once his proposal is adopted, he now becomes somewhat obligated to support the program himself!

A campaign against waste can thus become a *prospending* activity. It reinforces the assumption that government can and should handle the tasks it has undertaken. This is the approach of the General Accounting Office, for example, an approach that makes it part of the panoply of forces urging Congress to expand the size and scope of government.

The "waste" issue can be turned into an antispending argument, but it has to be properly marshaled. One has to make the case that waste is inherent in *any* government effort to handle the activity. In this illustration, the opponent of spending would argue that the failure of the school-lunch program to use soy extender in hamburgers illustrates how a massive, "no-bottom-line" bureaucracy will inevitably overlook efficiencies. Even if it managed to correct this instance of waste, the spending opponent would continue, there would be dozens more inefficiencies cropping up faster than outsiders could detect and correct them. Hence, the program should be terminated.

In conclusion, opposition to spending in general provides a shallow, ineffective basis for limiting spending. This is why efforts to limit spending through legal provisions have failed. They have attempted to implement a diffuse sentiment against spending, while leaving unquestioned the justifications for all the specific programs. It is the conviction that these specific programs are needed that drives the spending process and overpowers legal spending limitations. In effect, the legal approach ignores the existence of the culture of spending. It ignores the propaganda steamroller at work in Washington.

The effort to limit spending, if it is to succeed, must have a much deeper foundation than the diffuse idea that spending in general is "too high." It must marshal arguments against each specific spending program, profound arguments that say it is destructive and wrong for government to even attempt to solve the problem in question. In the following chapter, I will examine what this method of "program criticism" would mean in practice.

✦ 10 ✦

Countering the Culture: Program Criticism

TO CHECK GOVERNMENT SPENDING in a dependable, long-run fashion, the programs themselves must be criticized. The one-sided persuasion in favor of each program needs to be contradicted by contrary messages. Every time the congressman hears that a program is needed, he should also hear that it is not needed. Every time he hears that it is fair, he should also hear that it is unfair. Every time he hears that it is solving a problem, he should also be told that it is making problems worse.

This strategy of countering the culture of spending with antiprogram persuasion has not been advocated by any of the antispending forces. No one has taken up the idea of undermining the desire for spending by educating congressmen about the waste and harm of each program. A certain amount of program criticism does take place, of course, on those few budget items that shape up as major legislative battles. It is, however, largely a by-product of the effort to pass some type of lower-spending compromise measure—which means that the critiques are seldom profound or comprehensive.

Of course, an educational effort to criticize all federal programs would take enormous resources, for one is up against the billions spent by the government agencies and lobbyists in pro-program persuasion. This is not the reason why opponents of spending have little interest in this approach, however, for they are used to being outnumbered. Their resistance is based on philosophical points. In my explorations, I encountered three reasons why opponents of spending shy away from a systematic effort to criticize specific programs.

Is government our secret love? As we saw in the previous chapter, superficial criticisms of government programs simply invite "fix-it" responses that preserve programs or even cause their expansion. To mount an effective campaign of persuasion against a spending program, one has to argue that its failure goes very deep, so deep that it is incapable of being "fixed" simply by adding more spending or changing some rules. This means, in effect, that one has to argue that government is a deeply flawed problem-solving institution.

Most Americans, and certainly their politicians, do not accept this position. They have been raised in the cultural tradition that looks to government as the God-ordained manager and regulator of social life. They believe that government, apparently so wealthy and apparently so powerful, should fix whatever is wrong in society. Many see it as the *only* way of handling most of the problems we seem to face, being unaware that voluntary, noncoercive solutions are possible. Given this statist orientation, many reject analyses implying that government is inherently incompetent.

Several years ago, for example, an antispending group calling itself "Proposition One" was formed to speak out on the deficit. It was headed by a former governor of Vermont and had former presidents Gerald Ford and Jimmy Carter as honorary co-chairmen. Its advisory board contained eight former cabinet secretaries. This group of long-time government officials was understandably reluctant to consider that government is a flawed problem-solving institution. In its prepared statement delivered to a Senate appropriations subcommittee, it did not mention any failing or drawback in a single federal program. It confined its message to lamenting "the deficit" and urging a "balanced approach to the problem," including the adoption of tax increases.[1]

The question needs to be faced by antispending groups and by the American people: Is government a successful problem-solving institution? Those who believe the answer is "yes" are not, in the long run, opponents of spending.

The culture of antispending. The tactic of educating congressmen depends on personal contact with them. To succeed, the antispending lobbyist must try to establish a friendly rapport with the congressman. He must view the congressman as a reasonable, sincere person, someone worth trying to persuade.

Unfortunately, most antispending activists do not have this positive view. They see congressmen as selfish, mindlessly seeking their personal advantage and blind to the long-run welfare of the country. One leader in the antispending cause, a professor of economics, described congressmen as "a group of well-trained bandits." When I suggested he might be exaggerating, he insisted on this characterization. Asked why congressmen voted for spending, a lobbyist for another antispending organization replied that congressmen were "totally" preoccupied with their quest for reelection: "My explanation is that [to a congressman] public interest be damned, that only self-interest rules."

How this hostility develops is understandable. Just as most congressmen live in their highly reinforcing culture of spending, the antispending activists have their own subculture that reinforces the case against spending—a "culture of antispending." They read the *Wall Street Journal,* where the follies of government programs are chronicled. They subscribe to periodicals that deplore the actions of politicians. Many are graduates of right-leaning departments of economics where subsidies are seen as a form of crime.

Furthermore, those on this side of the political fence tend to have a highly skeptical turn of mind. They readily reject the manifest aspects of things, and are quick to strip away euphemism from the political process. When they apply this reductionism to spending, they see a system that closely resembles banditry: Selfish individuals hire lobbyists who "hire" politicians who use the force of the state to take money away from other people and give it to these selfish individuals. The corruption of this system seems so obvious to them that they assume it must be obvious to congressmen, too. This brings them to the cynical conclusion that legislators who participate in this process must themselves be corrupt, "well-trained bandits."

This interpretation has its appeal, but it is misguided. It underestimates how susceptible most people, including most congressmen, are to manifest appearances. Labels, packaging, illusions—these strongly affect most people. Congressmen tend to trust that government programs actually accomplish their intended purpose. They suppose that programs to "help farmers," or "help science," or "help the poor" actually do what they are intended to do. One has to work long and hard pointing out defects in each scheme to overcome this basic credulity.

The high-spending congressman does not feel he is a crook. He does not perceive that he is taking money away from some people to give it to others. He lives in a world of euphemism where the federal government "generates" a "general revenue" that well-intentioned "public servants" can spend to "promote the general welfare." The congressman's susceptibility to labels and appearances has one benefit, however: It means he is persuadable. His attitude can be affected by lobbyists who "package" the antispending position, who point out the negative aspects.

This congressman will not be persuaded by lobbyists who believe he is a dishonest cad. Persuasion depends on mutual respect and personal regard. This is the problem for many antispending activists. Having such a negative view of congressmen, they refuse even to approach them. If they do have an interview, or testify in a committee, they exude hostility—which provokes hostility in return. If antispending forces are to succeed in persuading congressmen against programs, they must establish the same degree of personal rapport with them as the prospending lobbyists now have. The first step in making these contacts is to overcome their hostile orientation toward high-spending congressmen.

The challenge of gradualism. One of the reasons why antispending activists I talked to were negative about the idea of persuading congressmen was their lack of success. They would point to an instance in which they had presented a view to a congressman in an interview, committee hearing, or letter, and failed to change the congressman's mind. One leader gave this perspective on testifying at committee hearings:

R: They're just not going to listen to you. I mean you're going to be wasting your breath. . . . Congressmen do not go into hearings with the idea, "Well, I'm going to learn about this." It comes back to the idea [stated earlier] that they're not there to make decisions for what they think is best for America. . . .

I've discovered that it is of such little value that the time you spend putting your testimony together and getting there on the Hill and so forth, your time can be much more productively spent. You can write probably five op eds [newspaper columns] in the same amount of time and send them out to hundreds of newspapers around the country, and if you've convinced fifteen readers, you've done more to help your cause than you have if you talk to a lot of deaf ears.

In being discouraged in their contacts with congressmen, activists are making two mistakes. First, it is unreasonable to suppose that anyone could, in a few minutes' presentation, actually change another's mind. The idea that an antispending advocate could convert a congressman in one contact is quite unrealistic. Look at the enormous forces one is up against. The congressman's opinion about spending programs is formed as the result of years of persuasion, persuasion that runs overwhelmingly in favor of almost all (nonmilitary) programs. On a typical program, the congressman would have received perhaps 10,000 prospending communications. How could one antispending message undo the influences of decades?

Although one message against spending would not produce a conversion, it can be expected to have *some* effect. This is the second error that antispending activists make in interpreting congressional reaction to their arguments. They assume that because they do not see a 180-degree change, they have failed completely. Generally this would not be so. Most people, especially politicians, respond not just to the merit of arguments but to their *mass*. The more they hear the same argument or position, the more they are persuaded to believe it. It is an almost physical process, a "Newtonian mechanics" of congressional persuasion.

The campaign to persuade congressmen to disapprove of specific spending programs is necessarily a long one, one in which each individual act of persuasion cannot be more than the proverbial drop in the bucket. It is because they sense this that many activists prefer to work for measures that will put a legal limit on overall spending. At first glance, these seem to be a way to check spending in a single stroke. The problem, as already explained, is that if congressmen continue to believe spending programs are needed and successful, they are likely to reject attempts to limit spending, or circumvent them if they are approved.

The strategy of educating congressmen about the defects of programs is undramatic and frustrating. It requires a long time and the efforts of many people. In the long run, however, it promises to address the spending problem at its roots.

Playing Christians and Lions

As part of the research for this book, I undertook to carry out the tactic of program criticism. What would happen, I wondered, to someone who approached Congress with criticisms of specific spending programs? How difficult was it to get a hearing? Would congressmen react violently when their favorite programs were denounced right in front of them?

My efforts centered on four appearances before appropriations subcommittees in 1988 and 1989. The programs I selected to criticize were the National Science Foundation, the federal feeding programs, especially food stamps, and agricultural research, especially agricultural policy research. In addition to the committee appearances, I also had an opportunity to assess the tactic of specific persuasion in my interviews with congressmen and staff where I raised antispending points and gauged their reaction. These contacts led to a number of observations about the congressional process that bear on the feasibility of the specific persuasion tactic.

Congress is open to communications from anyone. In attempting to contact congressmen and participate in the committee process, I was impressed by how open the congressional process is. Whatever their other failings, congressmen do not seal themselves off from the public. Of course, there are tremendous pressures for the time and attention of congressmen, congressional staff, and congressional committees, and these pressures mean that not everybody can get a hearing. The system aims at openness, however, and if you are persistent—and not hostile—you can eventually get a hearing wherever you want to be heard.

I was surprised to learn, for example, that the requirement for becoming a witness at a committee hearing is simply to ask. Of course, one needs to know whom to ask and when to ask, and one has to appear responsible, not a crank. The committees are willing to draw this line quite loosely. In my own case, I represented no organization and had no formal credentials concerning the specific programs on which I was testifying. I was simply a scholar who claimed to have something to say.

In all four subcommittees where I sought to make an appearance, I was scheduled and did appear. The crush of witnesses meant that no one testifying before the committee could receive much time, and I was rushed through along with everyone else. In one hearing, the 1988 appearance before the House Agriculture Appropriations Subcommittee, I was scheduled toward the end of the day's session and because the hearing was running late, I was given only about seventy seconds to state my case instead of the promised five minutes. This meant I did not have time to state a single argument against the spending in question (federal food programs). I protested this treatment in an article in the *Wall Street Journal*, which was subsequently reprinted in *Reader's Digest*. This generated constituent mail for the congressmen involved, which, in turn, helped me get a full, attentive hearing the following year.

In my contacts with the committees and with congressmen, I noticed how easy it would be for an opponent of spending to see antagonism and, in reaction, develop hostile attitudes toward congressmen. Time and again, for example, congressional aides would promise to phone me in connection with scheduling an interview and then break their promise. One begins to speculate about the devious motives that might lie behind the congressional evasion. I came to the conclusion, however, that the system is far less antagonistic than it appears. What it is, is *disorganized*. Congress is subject to such a crush of communications that it cannot possibly deal with them in an orderly way. As a result, it reacts to people and issues in a haphazard fashion. Once the lobbyist understands this— that he is dealing not with a purposeful institution but with a muddle—it is easier to keep one's patience and maintain a benevolent attitude.

Congressmen themselves are aware of the need for counterbalancing, program-questioning activity. The congressmen I talked to, even including those favoring high levels of spending, agreed that criticism of programs is not currently being presented to Congress, and they further agreed that it ought to be. I asked one high-spending House Democrat on the Agriculture Subcommittee of the Appropriations Committee how he would feel about witnesses who would testify against programs:

Q: As part of my whole study, I should tell you, I wanted to testify against some programs, because I felt, and members were telling me, that there really wasn't a balance, that the witnesses that would come in would be in favor of things.

R: Well, that's true. Everybody comes in attempting to defend a particular program. I think it's important to have the other perspective.

Q: You do?

R: Oh, sure.

Q: Well, I was wondering what your reaction would be.

R: I think it's important. We should be hearing a balanced view. The truth of the matter is that in each of these areas where subcommittees mark up bills, there is a danger and a tendency to have members of the subcommittee get a stake in particular parts of the bill.

Congressional aides feel the same way about the need for balance. When I mentioned to them that I planned to come to their committees and testify against spending, they were quite encouraging. Having grown cynical about the endless parade of witnesses saying "gimme, gimme," they saw the appearance of a program critic as a refreshing corrective.

Sources providing analyses and data for making the case against specific government programs are either unsuitable or nonexistent. In preparing my critiques of specific spending programs, I found that I had to do the job from scratch. To a large extent this was because no one had ever attempted *any* formal criticism of the spending in question. One of the spending programs I selected for criticism was the National Science Foundation. As far as I was able to ascertain, no one had ever written on "why funding the National Science Foundation is wrong." Indeed, I could not find even a single essay, scholarly or journalistic, on "why government funding of science is unsound." There has been plenty written on the NSF, its history, its accomplishments, how it could do a better job—even its mistakes. There is not one fundamental critique of the concept of having a governmental science-funding agency—even though, as I found, some devastating criticisms can be made (including the point that such an agency can retard the progress of science).

Another agency I criticized was the Economic Research Service of the Department of Agriculture. I chose it as an example of those scores of agencies that no one knows anything about and that keep getting funded year after year simply because their proposed mission sounds attractive at first glance. In the case of the ERS, no one—scholar or journalist—had written anything about it at all. To build my case, I had to interview people working in this agency. (I learned that the ERS functioned in direct contradiction to its announced mission. It is supposed to be an "honest mirror" evaluating government agricultural programs; to protect its funding, it systematically distorts or suppresses findings critical of these programs.)

Even on a program that had received public attention—food stamps—I found most of the published material unsuitable. For one thing, the journalistic accounts had relatively little dependable statistical data. The second problem was that the arguments against the program tended to be shallow. A commonly made point is that the food-stamp program is large, larger than people ever thought it would become. This point is hardly a criticism of the program, since one can always say that the "needs" are large. Another common objection, that the program contains some kind of "waste," or is not reaching the right beneficiaries, tends to be a pro-program argument: It implies the need for more spending to correct the flaws. No one, scholar or journalist, seems to have done a specific study on the really telling objections to the program. These objections would include the opportunity-cost issue (what citizens are giving up, in taxes, to fund the program), and motivational points (the effect of free food on the recipient's job-search behavior, family stability, and self-esteem).

If the tactic of program criticism is to be widely employed, more effort needs to go into profound antispending critiques.

In Congress, the attachment to spending is primarily cultural, not intellectual. The most surprising aspect of my congressional experiences is what did *not* happen. In all four appearances, I went before a congressional committee with a stern and comprehensive condemnation of a program that committee members had faithfully supported for years. Furthermore, I was the intruder. I was challenging these people on their home turf, in the sanctum sanctorum of the culture of spending, where they were surrounded by scores of lobbyists to cheer them on. Since I was contradicting what they believed in and worked for, I expected some kind of strong reaction, some defense of their beliefs, some criticism of my position. I assumed I had got myself into a game of Christians and lions and, in each committee, with considerable apprehension, I waited for the lions to start roaring.

They never did! No one was angry, no one was upset. Congressmen recognized that what I was saying was unusual, but their reaction was that they found it interesting, even something they tended to agree with. No one seemed to feel I was contradicting cherished beliefs.

This nonreaction was perhaps most striking at my second appearance before the House Agriculture Appropriations Subcommittee, where I criticized agricultural research programs. The stage for the confrontation was set by my previous year's appearance and the *Wall Street Journal / Reader's Digest* critiques. The committee members, including Chairman Whitten, had been sent copies of my testimony well in advance, along with cover letters explaining my intentions.

Since members of this committee, especially the chairman, have been faithful supporters of agricultural research spending, I expected a strong reaction. Looking straight at Rep. Whitten, I concluded my opening, oral statement with these words:

> The billions Congress is devoting to agricultural research are not buying solutions to our farm and rural problems. They are corrupting the independence of agricultural researchers and they are generating a clutter of biased and irrelevant output.
>
> Cutting back on these appropriations will not only save money, it will also enable us to see agricultural problems more clearly.[2]

Believing that I had just told a powerful septuagenarian that he had wasted his life in pursuit of error, I braced for a storm of abuse. It never came. Instead, Whitten was apologetic and hesitant. His first words were, "We appreciate your statement. I read ahead of you. You'd be surprised how many places I agree with you." He then went into a long, mumbling discourse on the many problems in the Department of Agriculture, and how he, too, had complained about them, and how little authority the appropriations committee had in these matters:

> The point I am making is that I agree with you; but we don't have the authority or the jurisdiction to correct it. Now what we do, and the things that you pointed out, I point out—to the degree I hear about them. I point them out because the first thing I try to do in an investigation is tell the agency so they can correct it. . . .
>
> I'll take pleasure in sending this [prepared statement] down to the Department [of Agriculture], to the Secretary. Now he's the man in charge of the Administration.[3]

Instead of lashing out, Rep. Whitten associated himself with the effort to criticize the Department of Agriculture. My testimony had triggered antispending perspectives and memories that momentarily displaced his prospending attitudes. Now his attention was focused on the point that government was, as he himself put it, "very wasteful." We see here a small illustration of how impressionable congressmen can be, how easily they react to and conform to those who are communicating with them. If thousands of similar antispending communications had been directed at Rep. Whitten over the ensuing days and years, would not a fiscal conservative be moldable out of this same congressional clay?

Of course, a single antispending presentation could not, and did not, produce a conversion. Whitten, at bottom, sensed that he was still a supporter of government agricultural research. This is why he adopted a "buck-passing" posture. Instead of offending me by saying that he didn't believe in a cut, he claimed powerlessness: The "real" decision maker was the secretary of agriculture.

Why was Rep. Whitten sparing my feelings? Why wasn't he angry with me for challenging his beliefs? Why did he allow my sweeping condemnation of cherished programs to stand in the committee record unchallenged? As I noted, this type of nonreaction was the pattern for all the congressmen in all the committees. They were hesitant and apologetic as I censured the very programs they seemingly believed in. What accounts for this curious behavior?

The answer is that, from their point of view, I was not challenging their *beliefs*. Their prospending attitudes had not been arrived at through an intellectual process, by examining evidence and weighing pros and cons. They were a *cultural prejudice*, an orientation passively absorbed from the social environment. Since this orientation was not "theirs" in an original, intellectual sense, they did not feel threatened or challenged when I criticized it.

For most congressmen, spending programs are cultural "givens," an aspect of their environment that they accept without question. They are, to a large extent, like clothing styles. Suppose, for example, someone went to Congress to testify against wearing the suit and tie and in favor of jeans and t-shirts. How would Rep. Whitten, who wears a suit and tie every day, respond? Would he feel personally challenged, and rush to refute the witness? No, because the challenge is not to his *personal beliefs*. Rep. Whitten didn't sit down one day and weigh the pros and cons of wearing a suit, and decide for himself what was right. He picked up this custom from his culture, and it is the culture that the witness is criticizing. Whitten has absorbed his orientation in favor of spending for agricultural research in the same way. It's what everyone around him tells him is normal and natural.

The cultural nature of most prospending attitudes has important implications for those who would oppose specific spending programs. On one hand, it means that the antispending message can get a hearing because the participants do not see it as a personal challenge. It also means that this message is not taken very seriously at first. The first time you tell a congressman that the National Science Foundation should not be funded, he reacts as if you told him he should be wearing jeans and a t-shirt. Your suggestion is weird and unrealistic. Only after many people have objected to funding can the matter become an intellectual issue, capable of being decided on its merits.

✦ 11 ✦

Countering the Culture: Term Limits

THE IDEA OF CONTROLLING the culture of spending with counterbalancing antispending communications is sound in theory, but it has a serious practical limitation: Who will do it? Antispending lobbyists are rare, and likely to remain so. I can testify from my own experience that it is a thankless job. It cost me a great deal of time and money, it was stressful and frustrating, and it defined me as an "outsider," thus impairing my career opportunities in government or in academia. It is not surprising that few people undertake this kind of activity.

The lack of program critics leads us to look to institutional changes, ways of changing how Congress is run that might have an effect in weakening the culture of spending. In the Appendix, "Reform Proposals," I have outlined a number of these possibilities. In my judgment, the most feasible and most effective reform would be a limitation on congressional terms.

Congressmen become indoctrinated to the prospending point of view through their long exposure to the highly one-sided persuasion in favor of government programs. As we saw in Chapter 5, the longer a congressman remains in Washington, the more complete is this socialization process. A limit on the congressional term would help counter the effects of this indoctrination, simply by preventing the more senior, dyed-in-the-wool program supporters from continuing in Congress.

176   *Controlling Spending*

We can get an idea of the effect of such a measure by comparing the voting behavior of junior and senior congressmen on spending issues. The term limitation commonly suggested for Congress is twelve years, that is, six terms for House members and two terms for senators. Using this as the dividing line between junior and senior congressmen, we find that this modest constitutional reform would have a significant impact on the fiscal orientation of Congress.

This point shows up quite clearly by using the National Taxpayer's Union ratings. The tabulation given in Table 11.1 shows that in the House of Representatives, the junior congressmen are always more fiscally conservative than the senior congressmen. (The year 1978 is chosen as the start of the series since that was when the NTU began basing its ratings on a comprehensive collection of spending measures.) This relationship holds in both parties: Senior

TABLE 11.1 Fiscal Conservatism of Junior and Senior Representatives, 1978–1989

	Average fiscal conservatism scores		
	Junior representatives	Senior representatives	Difference
1978	107	83	24
1979	103	92	11
1980	104	91	13
1981	103	91	12
1982	104	88	16
1983	104	87	17
1984	104	87	17
1985	104	88	16
1986	105	87	18
1987	107	84	23
1988	106	87	19
1989	103	94	9
Average	104.5	88.25	16.25

NOTE: Fiscal conservatism scores are computed from National Taxpayers Union ratings (where a higher score means the member voted for less spending). The NTU ratings have been adjusted so that the average rating for all House members in each year equals 100. Junior members are those who served six terms or fewer; senior members have served seven terms or more.

Democrats are bigger spenders than junior Democrats, and senior Republicans are bigger spenders than junior Republicans.[1]

The results for the Senate, given in Table 11.2, show the same pattern. The difference is not as marked, however, because most senators have already been long exposed to culture-of-spending influences before becoming senators. Almost all of them have had some government office, including that of U.S. representative, or state governor, or other state position. As in the House, the difference between junior and senior senators is found in both parties, although not as consistently.[2]

These two tables show that excluding members with over twelve years of service would result in a definite increase in fiscal conservatism of Congress. The budgetary implications of this change are difficult to estimate, but they would likely be quite significant. Even if the effect were only a few billion dollars less spending each year, the compound effect would be enormous. One billion dollars in savings in 1978, for example, would put spending growth

TABLE 11.2 Fiscal Conservatism of Junior and Senior Senators, 1978–1989

	Average fiscal conservatism scores		
	Junior senators	Senior senators	Difference
1978	103	93	10
1979	105	89	16
1980	102	94	8
1981	103	92	11
1982	103	92	11
1983	104	90	14
1984	101	97	4
1985	101	98	3
1986	100	100	0
1987	102	95	7
1988	99	101	–2
1989	103	95	8
Average	102.2	94.7	7.5

NOTE: Fiscal conservatism scores are computed from National Taxpayers Union ratings (where a higher score means the member voted for less spending). The NTU ratings have been adjusted so that the average rating for all senators in each year equals 100. Junior members are those who served twelve years or fewer; senior members have served thirteen years or more.

on a lower curve and result in a budget $10 or $20 billion lower a decade later. If added to this one billion dollars in savings in 1978 there were additional savings (less spending growth) in 1979, and again in 1980, and so on, the compound effect on the 1990 budget could have been hundreds of billions of dollars less spending. In other words, the more fiscally conservative Congress created by the term-limitation amendment, had it been adopted in, say, 1978, would probably have meant a balanced federal budget in 1990.

The picture given by the NTU spending scores is reinforced by the voting patterns on other budgetary decisions. For example, on July 17, 1990, the House voted on a proposed balanced-budget amendment to the Constitution (H.J.R. 268). The idea of this measure is to limit spending growth by requiring a balanced budget. As I argued in Chapter 9, it is doubtful that such a provision would really limit spending, but congressmen reacted to it as if it would. The vote therefore reflects sentiment toward the idea of limiting the size of the federal government. All but five Republicans voted in favor of the amendment, so a junior-senior comparison is not possible for that party. The Democrats, however, divided on the issue, giving us a chance to test the effect of seniority on the vote. The results, given in Table 11.3, show a clear seniority effect. The longer they have served in Congress, the more hostile Democratic members are to the idea of a constitutional balanced budget amendment.

This proposed amendment, incidentally, fell seven votes short of the necessary two-thirds majority and therefore was defeated. Had a term-limitation provision been in effect, eliminating the big-

---

TABLE 11.3 Seniority and Democratic Representatives' Votes on the Balanced Budget Amendment (July 17, 1990)

Number of terms served	Percentage of representatives voting against amendment
One	30
Two and three	39
Four and five	58
Six and seven	64
Eight or more	69

NOTE: The number of representatives in each category is as follows: one term = 23; two and three terms = 41; four and five terms = 72; six and seven terms = 45; eight terms or more = 74. On this measure, all but five Republicans voted in favor.

spending senior Democrats from the picture, it would have passed with scores of votes to spare.

Another critical budget decision was the five-year budget plan approved by Congress on October 27, 1990. This was the agreement worked out between President Bush and congressional leaders to avoid the automatic budget restraints implied in the Gramm-Rudman-Hollings Act. The budget package shocked the nation by purporting to "cut" the budget while actually increasing non-defense spending by at least $245 billion. To pay for this increased spending, the plan effectively dismantled the Gramm-Rudman-Hollings Act and the fiscal discipline implied therein; it increased taxes by $137.2 billion; and it provided—in what was billed as a "deficit reduction package"—for an increase in the deficit, to a record $254 billion for 1991.[3] To outside observers, it seemed an arrangement to insure the growth of government spending at all costs.

If the constitutional term-limitation amendment had been in effect, this budget plan would not have been approved, for it was senior members, those serving more than twelve years, who gave it the margin of victory. In the House, the measure passed by twenty-eight votes, 228–220; with the senior members removed, it would have failed by four votes, 142–146. In the Senate, the measure passed by nine votes, 54–45. With the exclusion of the senior members, it would have failed by six votes, 26–32.

In addition to the direct effect of the term-limitation amendment in producing a more fiscally conservative Congress, this reform would have an indirect effect. The big-spending senior congressmen have an influence in Congress that goes beyond casting their own vote. They are the leadership members who chair the committees and control the agenda, and thus influence the policy-making process in many ways. In discussing the "apprenticeship effect" in Chapter 5, we noted how freshman congressmen are drawn to vote more in favor of spending programs than they otherwise would, out of their desire to conform to leadership positions.

We can gauge the importance of this leadership effect by examining the most important congressional leader of all, the speaker of the House, currently the leader of the Democratic majority. It is widely known that the speaker is a senior Democratic congressman. It is less well known, however, that in modern times the speaker reflects the extreme prospending wing of the Democratic party. The current House speaker, Democrat Thomas Foley of Washington, had National Taxpayers Union ratings much lower than the average Democrat in the years before he became speaker. (Since the speaker rarely votes on any measure, valid spending scores for incumbent speakers cannot be compiled.) For example, in 1988, the year before Foley became speaker, House Democrats had an average NTU rating of 20, while Foley's rating was an extremely low 14.

The pattern was the same for Jim Wright of Texas, the previous speaker. Even though from a presumably "conservative" state, Wright's NTU scores were far below even the Democratic average in the years before he became speaker. In 1986, just before he became speaker, the Democratic average score was 29, while Wright's was 18, a score identifying him as the eighth biggest spender in the entire 435-member House of Representatives. In recent times, any congressman concerned about "not offending the speaker" will be drawn in a prospending direction.

A limitation on congressional terms, then, would not only eliminate the votes of militant big-spending senior members from Congress, but would also eliminate their prospending leadership influence.

We see that term limitation, a seemingly modest institutional reform, could have a profound impact in limiting spending. It would be too optimistic to expect it to accomplish a major reversal in the size of government, for the attitudes underlying the modern, all-encompassing welfare state are quite widespread. Furthermore, as we noted in Chapter 5, prospending socialization can affect legislators before they come to Congress, since many have served as congressional aides or state legislators, for example. Nevertheless, this reform promises to be of definite use in restraining the growth of government spending.

One of the main arguments given against congressional term limitation is that it would strengthen lobbyists and agency officials. "Term limitation, by removing years of expertise from Capitol Hill, would increase the power of the permanent bureaucracy," says one critic.[4] "Power would flow from elected to unelected officials," says another.[5] "This would only make the bureaucracy more powerful," says a third.[6]

Those adopting this view do not offer any evidence to document their speculations. As we have just noted, the data indicate the converse is true. Even a hasty glance should have told these commentators that something was wrong with their theory. All over Capitol

Hill, federal bureaucracies and their spending programs are being preserved and promoted by senior congressmen—such as twenty-five-term Jamie Whitten.

The popularity of this misleading idea is an important comment on the current approach to theorizing about politics. *It is an approach that ignores the impact of persuasion on politicians.* Anyone who considered the persuasion process could never make the mistake of supposing that senior congressmen would be opponents of bureaucracy. The logic is obvious: Congressmen are persuaded on the basis of what they hear; most of what congressmen hear comes, directly and indirectly, from the government agencies; therefore, the longer a congressman stays in Washington, the more he will come to agree with the position of the bureaucracy. Observers miss this elementary conclusion because they ignore the premise, the notion that congressmen are persuaded on the basis of what they hear.

Needed: A Second Madisonian Revolution

When the Constitution was drawn up in 1787, the founding fathers were preoccupied with the problem of tyranny. What was to prevent one group or faction from gaining control of the government and setting up a dictatorship? Today, we face a similar problem of unchecked power. The expansion of government has generated bureaucracies and beneficiary groups that put forth a one-sided account of government action. They supply a broad stream of propaganda in favor of government programs. This progovernment propaganda represents a form of power. Unchecked, it fosters the continuous growth of government at the expense of private, voluntary action.

The limitation of congressional terms affords a simple way to begin to limit this power. It is worth remembering that in the early days of this country, long before bureaucracies gained their current abilities to indoctrinate public officials, extended service in government was considered unhealthy. Officials were expected to limit their service, and, for the most part, they did. It was felt that the continued exposure to the government perspective would induce public officials to love government more than the people they were supposed to serve. This argument applies with redoubled force today.

Appendix

Fallacies of
Cost–Benefit Analysis

IN PRINCIPLE, cost–benefit analysis should be a useful tool in helping policy makers decide on the merit of governmental expenditures. If a program delivers benefits worth more than the program costs, then one could say it is a worthwhile, desirable program. If the costs of a program outweigh the benefits, then obviously policy makers should abandon it.

In partisan hands, however, cost–benefit analysis is simply a tool of advocacy. Agencies seeking to defend their programs distort the results by understating costs and by exaggerating benefits. Two major errors characterize virtually every use of cost–benefit analysis, from highly quantitative findings elaborated by trained economists and accountants to informal claims of politicians.

The failure to include the cost of tax collection. Cost–benefit analyses typically assume that government funds are raised without cost. In fact, the collecting of taxes imposes a huge burden on Americans and the American economy. These costs include the cost of funding the IRS and other government agencies involved in administering the tax system, compliance costs (recordkeeping, learning about the tax code, preparing forms), enforcement costs (responding to IRS computer accusations, audits, penalties, collection actions, and participating in tax litigation), evasion and avoidance costs, and disincentive costs. Finally, there are many emotional and moral costs, ranging from the anxiety the tax system creates to the inculcation of dishonest habits. A comprehensive estimate of the monetary costs alone puts these at 65 cents for each tax dollar collected.[1] Whatever the precise estimate, the general point is inescapable: taxpayer dollars do not float into the Treasury with no inconvenience and without social cost. Cost–benefit analyses that assume otherwise contain a blatant bias in favor of governmental action.

The failure to match public benefits against private benefits for the use of the same funds. As cost–benefit analysis is practiced today, much effort and imagination goes into stipulating the indirect benefits of a particular governmental expenditure. An analyst defending an infant nutrition program, for example, will assert that the program keeps children from getting sick and include as a "benefit" the reduction in hospital bills. The omission in this approach is the analyst's failure to consider the benefits of the same funds if left in private hands. The implicit assumption is that when a dollar is spent by the federal government, it has a multitude of wonderful and multiplying indirect benefits, but when left in the hands of an ordinary American, it remains limp and lifeless, bringing no more than one dollar of benefit to the holder.

Obviously, this is a profoundly progovernment assumption. The private expenditure of funds also brings indirect and accumulating benefits both to the individual and to society. The money a mother spends to buy a sweater for her infant, for example, will improve that infant's health, thus resulting in reduced medical costs, and so forth. In other words, a dollar privately held and privately spent will have a benefit/cost ratio greater than 1. To justify a federal spending program, therefore, it is not enough to show that the benefit/cost ratio exceeds 1. What must be demonstrated is that the benefit/cost ratio for the public expenditure exceeds that for the private expenditure of the same dollar. If an analyst is highly inventive in listing "benefits" of federal programs, then to be fair he must be equally inventive in stating the benefits of the same dollar retained and spent privately.

Making these public–private comparisons is difficult, of course, because we don't know *which* private dollar is going into the federal program we are analyzing. For example, one could claim that the dollars spent on a federal nutrition program came, in the form of taxes, from self-employed inventors. One could argue that these dollars, left in the hands of the inventors to support their research, would create inventions worth a thousand times as much to society. Under this assumption, the federal nutrition program should be cancelled, since its benefit/cost ratio would never approach 1,000.

One way to relate public and private efficiencies is to adopt a "public–private matching" technique, comparing the governmental program to the private expenditures for the same purpose. A federal nutrition program, for example, would be seen as taking private funds devoted to nutrition—that is, funds that individuals would have spent purchasing nutritious foods and nutrition supplements, or taking nutrition courses, or buying nutrition books.

This matching technique will produce a rather disappointing conclusion about the value of government action in most domestic programs. It shows that in many cases the public spending program is merely duplicating private action, but with numerous inefficiencies. Take the nutrition example. A governmental feeding/nutrition program would tend to have identical benefits that private feeding/nutrition expenditures have: illness prevented, children more productive at school, and so on. But the government program would involve the additional overhead costs of tax collection and the costs and wastes inherent in governmental management and administration.

To offer another application of public–private matching, consider government job-training programs. All sorts of benefits have been claimed for these programs, from increasing government tax revenues to reducing crime. There are, however, private job-training "programs," ranging from the programs of large corporations to informal apprenticeships between individual workers. These programs would be expected to have at least the same benefits as federal job-training programs: more productive workers, less crime, less illness, more tax revenues. Since the benefit/cost ratio for both programs would be the same, there would be no justification for taking funds from private job-training programs and shifting them to the public ones, thus incurring the collection and disbursement costs inherent in federal action.

The cost–benefit analyst may not agree with this public–private matching technique. It is, after all, only a tool, and perhaps other techniques for recognizing the benefits of private action would work better. But what the analyst *cannot* do is assume that money spent by government has indirect and multiplying benefits while assuming that the same money left in private hands has no such benefits. This is, today, the approach to cost–benefit analysis as practiced by politicians and by consulting firms. That this fallacy should be so widespread illustrates how the imperatives of the culture of spending have undermined sound reasoning.

Measuring
Congressional Spending

IN DEVISING A MEASURE of congressmen's orientation toward spending, one must first decide which purpose is to be served, evaluation or explanation.

A measure aimed at evaluating congressmen should include all votes bearing on spending of whatever type, and should weight those votes according to their importance in adding to spending. This is the type of measure that has been developed by the National Taxpayers Union, which bases its scores on all votes affecting spending and weights each of these votes according to the judgments of a panel of congressmen on the relative importance of each vote in adding to spending. This measure is designed to answer the question, Whom should we *blame* for spending?

A different purpose for a spending measure is *explanation*—that is, testing different theories about *why* congressmen vote for spending. That is the aim of the spending measure developed in this study. I began with an inventory of all 219 House roll call votes for 1986 bearing on spending, supplied by David Keating of the National Taxpayers Union. First, the military spending votes were set aside to form a separate military spending score. Since support for military spending correlates inversely with support for all other spending, the two do not "belong" in the same scale. Any theory of why congressmen vote for spending must recognize that there are two separate kinds of spending.

Since we are concerned with why congressmen spend and not the consequences of spending in terms of the size of the budget, we do not need to weight votes according to the size of spending involved. In effect, we aim at a scale that measures a congressman's *disposition to spend*. This disposition to spend is not related to the amount of spending involved in the particular vote. An analogy with personal finances will help clarify the point. We would not call someone a "spendthrift" if he paid his $600 mortgage payment, but we would apply that term to someone who spent $6 on dessert at a restaurant. It is not the amount spent that reveals a person's disposition to spend, but the degree of necessity or avoidability in the expenditure. The "big spender" is someone who purchases the nonessential extras.

How can we gauge the relative "avoidability" of a particular spending vote? An objective method is to let the participants indicate this by their division or consensus on the item. The fact that virtually everybody makes a mortgage payment indicates that it is a relatively unavoidable expenditure. By the same logic, unanimous or near unanimous spending votes imply an inexorable quality to the item. When there is a split vote, on the other hand, this implies that the expenditure is more in the nature of a "dessert"—something not so clearly compelled by circumstances. One principle of selecting votes for this measure, then, is that they must be nonunanimous votes, with at least 20 percent of the congressmen voting on the losing side.

Although many bills have some implications for spending, to maintain the purity of the spending measure it is important to confine attention to those votes where spending is the *main and direct implication*—of the vote. On many measures, such as legislation that changes the operation of a program, the implication for spending is indirect; these are excluded. Falling in the same category are votes dealing with budget procedure, budget targets, and procedural reform. These votes do not necessarily and directly have an impact on spending. Also excluded are votes in which the spending issue is entangled in highly complex parliamentary procedures so that the spending aspect is not directly visible. A vote is also excluded when the spending aspect involves a separate policy point, such as a spending vote on the abortion controversy.

Another category of votes set aside is the votes on final passage of general spending measures—that is, major budget bills and continuing resolutions. These bills, being so large and so noticeable, may seem to represent dramatic spending votes, but this is misleading. A major budget bill is the result of a long process of legislative decision making. It is the summation of many amendments and test votes on separate items. When the time comes to vote on the entire thing, the vote is more a vote to expedite the budget process than a vote for or against spending. It tends to be rather *pro forma*. Furthermore, the final bill may well contain spending cuts (achieved through separate votes on prior amendments). Hence, the opponents of spending might be eager to get the final bill passed so as to "lock in" these cuts.

Finally, to avoid duplication, when two or more votes are taken on the same spending item, only one vote is used, the one that produced the closest split. The source employed for both the descriptions of the bills and the votes of congressmen is Congressional Quarterly's *Weekly Report*.

The application of these decision rules reduced the original 219 spending-related votes to 41, with 36 nonmilitary spending votes for the general spending score and 5 military spending votes for the separate military spending score. For the most part, these votes involved the authorization or appropriation of higher or lower spending amounts for specific programs. The general (nonmilitary) spending votes are listed as follows (the numbers in parentheses refer to Congressional Quarterly 1986 House roll call votes):

Health and safety
- Consumer Product Safety Commission (CQ 18)
- Bubonic plague program (CQ 81)

Antipoverty/low income assistance
- Community and migrant health centers (CQ 22)
- Indian health care programs (CQ 90)
- Follow Through program (CQ 92)
- Community Services Block Grant program (CQ 93)
- Labor, Health and Human Services, and Education, cap on increases (CQ 249)

Public works, construction, and transportation
- Construction of eight Energy Dept. research facilities (CQ 216)
- Appalachian Regional Commission (CQ 219)

- Energy and water appropriations (CQ 221)
- Amtrack funding level (CQ 241)
- Department of Transportation, fractional reduction (CQ 245)
- Los Angeles mass transit (CQ 277)
- Salinity research laboratory (CQ 401)

Business

- Trust fund for companies harmed by imports (CQ 121)
- Urban Development Action Grant program (CQ 130)
- Economic Development Administation (CQ 204)
- Loans to nondisadvantaged small businesses (CQ 207)

Agriculture

- Department of Agriculture, fractional reduction (CQ 229)
- Wheat subsidy payments (CQ 428)

Public housing

- Benefits for specific housing projects (CQ 132)
- Rent reduction in elderly housing (CQ 140)
- Funding for specific housing projects (CQ 147)

General government

- Departments of Commerce, Justice, State, and Judiciary appropriations, fractional reduction (CQ 209)
- District of Columbia appropriations (CQ 225)
- Treasury and Postal Service appropriations (CQ 268)
- Grants to state and local law enforcement agencies (CQ 341)
- Creation of advisory commission on the comprehensive education of intercollegiate athletes (CQ 347)

Legislative branch spending

- House committee staff funding (CQ 233)
- Phase out fourteen elevator operators (CQ 234)
- Overall legislative branch appropriations, fractional reduction (CQ 235)

Miscellaneous measures

- Federal crime insurance program (CQ 133)
- VISTA reauthorization (CQ 154)
- Legal Services Corporation (CQ 206)
- Philippines aid authorization (CQ 279)
- Enhance Columbia River Gorge (CQ 445)

The military spending votes are as follows:

- Defense budget, fractional reduction (CQ 285)
- MX missile (CQ 289)
- Bradley troop carrier (CQ 293)
- SDI funding level (CQ 300)

In scoring the votes, a congressman was given one point for each vote in which he voted on the higher spending side, zero for each vote on the lower spending side, and 0.5 for an absence. If a congressman had more than 10 absences in the 41 votes, he was dropped from the analysis. The application of this rule leaves us with a total of 414 congressmen for whom valid scores were compiled. Table A1 gives the correlations between the different subcomponents of the 36-vote general spending score, as well as the correlation of each of these against the military spending score. These figures document two general propositions about voting for spending: On all types of spending except military, there is a consistency or homogeneity in voting patterns; and voting for military spending is inversely associated with voting for all other types of spending.

Table A2 gives the correlations between my spending measures and other measures. It shows, first, that there is a high correlation between my (nonmilitary) spending measure and the NTU spending measure. (Since the NTU scores are "antispending" scores, with higher numbers reflecting voting against spending, the correlation with our scores is negative, $r = -0.92$.) Although NTU scores include military spending votes, these form a rather small part of the whole score, hence the NTU scores amount to a general nonmilitary spending measure.

The table also shows that ADA ratings match general spending scores quite closely ($r = +0.88$), and that Democratic party affiliation is positively correlated with general spending ($r = +0.83$), and negatively correlated with military spending ($r = -0.67$).

TABLE A1 Correlation of Spending Subscores

	Health	Anti-poverty	Public works	Business	Agri-culture	Housing	Govern-ment	Legislature	Misc.	General[a]
Health										
Antipoverty	.83									
Public works	.67	.79								
Business	.71	.82	.78							
Agriculture	.42	.46	.56	.45						
Housing	.78	.85	.77	.82	.46					
Government	.71	.77	.77	.68	.49	.73				
Legislative	.75	.81	.78	.72	.48	.75	.78			
Miscellaneous	.83	.89	.73	.77	.39	.82	.76	.78		
General[a]	.85	.94	.90	.88	.57	.90	.87	.89	.91	
Military	-.69	-.71	-.52	-.56	-.30	-.61	-.57	-.61	-.72	-.69

a. 36-vote general spending score.

TABLE A2   Correlation between Spending Scores and Other Measures

	Party[a]	ADA	NTU	General spending score
ADA rating	.78			
NTU score	−.76	−.73		
General spending score	.83	.88	−.92	
Military spending score	−.67	−.85	.48	−.69

a. Party is scored as a dichotomous variable, R = 0, D = 1.

Reform Proposals

PROPOSING REFORMS is a little like going window-shopping. Most of what we see is not really practical, or within our budget, or suitable for our tastes, but the experience is stimulating. It is in this spirit that I advance these reforms. I hope to stimulate the reader's imagination about the possibilities for countering the culture of spending. These proposals also serve to illustrate points made in this book: Stating remedies helps to clarify the diagnosis.

Since these suggestions are intended as thought exercises, I do not discuss the possible objections to them nor work out their specific forms for adoption. They are not fanciful, however: If readers wanted to counter the culture of spending, these ideas could be put in operational form, and would—to varying degrees—help limit spending. Many of the reforms proposed here are aimed at influencing the intellectual climate rather than changing the political process. That is, the purpose of these reforms is not so much to force politicians to do something differently but to provoke them to view their actions in a light that would lead to less spending.

Create Balanced Institutions

Form private organizations to foster criticism of specific spending programs. These would be groups whose announced mission is to bring to light the disadvantages of government programs so that Congress and the public could make an informed decision about them.

They would assemble information, sources, and personnel useful in criticizing specific government programs, would compile critiques of specific programs, and would provide these critiques to congressmen, congressional staff, and the press.

Form a governmental unit with the same function. This office would supply Congress and the public with information about the disadvantages of federal programs—thus counterbalancing the prospending arguments of the agencies. This is a Madisonian solution of contriving a branch of government to check or counteract others. The challenge, of course, is how to create a government agency that remains a thoroughgoing opponent of government action. The examples of the Office of Management and Budget and the General Accounting Office illustrate the difficulty.

Counter Prospending Lobbyists in Hearings

Adopt a resolution urging balanced committee hearings. The possible language is as follows:

> Considering that responsible decisions about the use of public funds can best be made by hearing testimony both for and against the respective program;
> And that opponents of programs typically go unrepresented or underrepresented in the hearing process;
> Be it resolved that the [committee, chamber] declares its desire to hear from responsible opponents of federal programs when these are considered in the hearings process, and directs chairmen and committee staff to encourage the participation of such opponents of federal programs in all relevant hearings.

Adopt an equal-time rule in committee hearings. In the consideration of all program authorizations or appropriations, the time for testimony should be divided equally between supporters of the program (including agency personnel) and opponents of the program.

Return to the system of closed hearings, with press and lobbyists excluded when administrators are testifying.

Ban congressmen from testifying as witnesses in congressional commit-tees. The purpose of a congressional hearing is to gather information from the outside so that congressmen may be better informed. For congressmen to attempt to learn about the world by listening to each other suggests incestuousness in the information-gathering process, a true "house without windows."

Ban witnesses from testifying before the same committee two years in a row.

Limit Indoctrination Effects

Limit the term of service for congressmen.

Prohibit former House members from serving in the Senate.

Prohibit former employees of government agencies from becoming a member of Congress. Anyone who has been employed by the federal government for a total of more than five years in any capacity would be ineligible to be a U.S. representative or senator.

Limit the length of time a congressman can serve on any committee.

Limit the Abuse of the Policy Evaluation Process

As shown in Chapter 2, policy evaluation has become a national scandal, with hundreds of millions of federal dollars being used to produce biased analysis in support of federal programs. Legislation to check abuses might include a law to:

Prohibit federal agencies from commissioning evaluations or cost–benefit analyses of their own programs. A different approach would be to try to rescue the evaluation idea by making it less biased in favor of federal spending programs:

Require that all program evaluations or cost–benefit analyses must be carried out by a research group that includes self-declared opponents of the program in question.

Require that all program evaluations or cost–benefit analyses include the social cost of raising funds for the program through the tax system. On the basis of the appropriate studies, the Office of Management and Budget could announce what figure should be used (see the Appendix, "Fallacies of Cost–Benefit Analysis").

Require that all evaluations or cost-benefit analyses of government programs include all the indirect and cumulative benefits that would accrue from the private expenditure of the funds (see the Appendix, "Fallacies of Cost–Benefit Analysis").

Counter the Presumption of Governmental Efficacy and the Philanthropic Fallacy

Require that all spending measures contain wording explicitly recognizing the fallibility of government action. Suggested language to appear in the preamble to every bill:

> The Congress recognizes that, in the past, government programs to remedy problems have in many cases failed, being characterized by misconceived purposes, waste, mismanagement, corruption, and negative unintended side effects.
>
> However, the Congress judges that in the case of monies spent for [program], any problems of misconceived purposes, waste, mismanagement, corruption, or negative unintended side effects will be exceeded by the benefits of the program.

This language might have little effect on programs at first, but it would give journalists something to point to years later ("you promised this wouldn't happen"), and thus help gradually to wean everyone—legislators and the public—from the presumption that programs accomplish their intended purposes.

Require that spending measures contain wording explicitly noting the public–private trade-off. Suggested language:

> The Congress recognizes that in authorizing this expenditure, it is taking monies from American citizens who have important and valid uses for their funds. However, Congress judges that

monies spent in [program] bring a greater advantage to the American people than would accrue if these same funds were left in the hands of individuals to spend for their own needs and purposes.

This language would probably not change any actual legislative outcomes in the short run. But in the long run, it would help erode the assumption made by congressmen and lobbyists that federal dollars are "free."

Even to propose adding language such as this to just one bill would probably provoke an interesting and educational debate.

Notes

Chapter 1

1. *Dollars and Sense* (Washington, D.C.: National Taxpayers Union, October/November 1987), p. 2.

2. See Bruce L. Gardner, *The Governing of Agriculture* (Lawrence: Regents Press of Kansas, 1981); Don Paarlberg, *Farm and Food Policy* (Lincoln: University of Nebraska Press, 1980); Joel Solkoff, *The Politics of Food* (San Francisco: Sierra Club Books, 1985); E. C. Pasour, Jr., *Agriculture and the State: Bureaucracy and the Market Process* (New York: Holmes & Meier, 1989); Michael Fumento, "Some Dare Call Them Robber Barons," *National Review*, March 13, 1987, pp. 32–38; James Bovard, "Feeding Everybody: How Federal Food Programs Grew and Grew," *Policy Review* 26 (Fall 1983), pp. 42–51; Karl Zinsmeister, "Plowing under Subsidies," *Reason*, October 1989, pp. 30–37; Don Paarlberg, "Tarnished Gold: Fifty Years of New Deal Farm Programs," *Imprimis* 16, no. 11 (November 1987); Robert L. Thompson, "Agriculture: Growing Government Control," in David Boaz, ed., *Assessing the Reagan Years* (Washington, D.C.: Cato Institute, 1988); William Tucker, "Why Farm Subsidies Have Come a Cropper," *Reader's Digest*, January 1987, pp. 81–86.

3. The statement from which the quotations are drawn appears in *Agricultural Credit Conditions* (Hearings before the Subcommittee on Conservation, Credit, and Rural Development of the Committee on Agriculture, House of Representatives, 99th Congress, 1st Session), pp. 270–73.

4. Ibid., p. 991.

5. *Private Sector Initiatives to Feed America's Poor* (Hearing before the Committee on Agriculture, Nutrition, and Forestry, Senate, 98th Congress, 1st Session), p. 28.

6. Ibid., p. 45.

7. Only those witnesses who physically appeared at the hearing are included in the tabulation. Witnesses who submitted written statements and letters but did not actually appear are not included.

Witnesses who were physically present but did not speak, or speak significantly, are credited for the position (prospending, antispending, or neutral) taken by the other witnesses in the group with which they appeared. Thus, they are coded with the position that congressmen would perceive them to have.

Witnesses who appeared before the committee on more than one session are recounted as witnesses for each session in which they appeared.

The full titles of each hearing are :

Agriculture/Food programs: *Rural Development, Agriculture, and Related Agencies Appropriations for 1988* (Hearings before a subcommittee of the Committee on Appropriations, House of Representatives, 100th Congress, 1st Session).

Housing/Space/Science: *Department of Housing and Urban Development—Independent Agencies Appropriations for 1988* (Hearings before a subcommittee of the Committee on Appropriations, House of Representatives, 100th Congress, 1st Session).

Farm credit: *Agricultural Credit Conditions* (Hearings before the Subcommittee on Conservation, Credit, and Rural Development of the Committee on Agriculture, House of Representatives, 99th Congress, 1st Session).

Appraisal of research: *Appraisal of Title XIV (Research) Agriculture Act of 1977* (Hearing before the Subcommittee on Department Investigations, Oversight, and Research of the Committee on Agriculture, House of Representatives, 95th Congress, 2nd Session).

Job training: *The Job Corps: Do Its Benefits Outweigh the Costs?* (Hearing before a subcommittee of the Committee on Government Operations, House of Representatives, 99th Congress, 1st Session).

Job training: *Job Corps Oversight Hearing* (Hearing before the Subcommittee on Employment Opportunities of the Committee on Education and Labor, House of Representatives, 99th Congress, 2nd Session).

Diplomatic security: *The Diplomatic Security Program* (Hearings and markup before the Committee on Foreign Affairs, Subcommittee on International Operations of the House of Representatives, 99th Congress).

Agriculture/Food programs: *Agriculture, Rural Development, and Related Agencies Appropriations for Fiscal Year 1988* (Hearings before a subcommittee of the Committee on Appropriations, United States Senate, 100th Congress, 1st Session).

Housing/NASA: *Department of Housing and Urban Development and Certain Independent Agencies Appropriations for Fiscal Year 1988* (Hearings before a subcommittee of the Committee on Appropriations, United States Senate, 100th Congress, 1st Session).

Farm credit: *Examination of the Financial Condition of the Farm Credit System* (Hearings before the Committee on Agriculture, Nutrition, and Forestry, United States Senate, 99th Congress, 1st Session).

Private-sector feeding efforts: *Private Sector Initiatives to Feed America's Poor* (Hearing before the Committee on Agriculture, Nutrition, and Forestry, United States Senate, 98th Congress, 1st Session).

Job training: *Job Training Partnership Act Amendments of 1986* (Hearing before the Subcommittee on Employment and Productivity of the Committee on Labor and Human Resources, United States Senate, 99th Congress, 2nd Session).

Volunteers/ACTION programs: *Reauthorization of the Domestic Volunteer Service Act of 1973* (Hearing before the Subcommittee on Children, Family, Drugs and Alcoholism of the Committee on Labor and Human Resources, United States Senate, 99th Congress, 2nd Session).

Foreign aid: *A.I.D. Oversight* (Hearings before the Committee on Foreign Relations, United States Senate, 99th Congress, 2nd Session).

8. For 1986, the Select Committee on Aging (and its subcommittees) held 33 percent of its meetings outside Washington; the Committee on Education and Labor (and its subcommittees) held 27 percent of its meetings outside Washington;

the Committee on Ways and Means (and its subcommittees) held 9 percent of its meetings outside Washington; the Committee on Agriculture (and its subcommittees) held 7 percent of its meetings outside Washington. Compiled from *Monthly Catalog of United States Government Publications*, Cumulative Index 1986 (Washington, D.C.: Government Printing Office, 1986).

9. *Congressional Record*, 100th Congress, 1st Session, (February 19, 1987), pp. HL 89–139. This is the quarterly report of the Clerk of the House and the Secretary of the Senate on lobbyists registered with Congress.

10. Robert H. Salisbury and Paul Johnson, "Who You Know versus What You Know: The Uses of Government Experience for Washington Lobbyists," *American Journal of Political Science* 33 (February 1989), p. 178.

11. James T. Bennett and Thomas J. DiLorenzo, *Destroying Democracy; How Government Funds Partisan Politics* (Washington, D.C.: Cato Institute, 1985).

12. Howard E. Shuman, *Politics and the Budget* (Englewood Cliffs, N.J.: Prentice-Hall, 1984), p. 70.

13. Robert Higgs, Crisis and Leviathan (New York: Oxford University Press, 1987).

14. *Agricultural Credit Conditions*, p. 29.

15. *Department of Housing and Urban Development—Independent Agencies Appropriations for 1988* (Hearings before a subcommittee of the Committee on Appropriations, House of Representatives, 100th Congress, 1st Session), part 4, p. 1.

16. *Agriculture, Rural Development, and Related Agencies Appropriations for 1987* (Hearings before a subcommittee of the Committee on Appropriations, House of Representatives, 99th Congress, 2nd Session), part 4, p. 406.

17. Ibid., part 5, p. 1.

18. *Rural Development, Agriculture, and Related Agencies Appropriations for 1988* (Hearings before a subcommittee of the Committee on Appropriations, House of Representatives, 100th Congress, 1st Session), part 2, p. 48.

19. *The Washington Post*, October 27, 1987.

Chapter 2

1. *Agriculture, Rural Development, and Related Agencies Appropriations for 1987* (Hearings before a subcommittee of the Committee on Appropriations, House of Representatives, 99th Congress, 2nd Session), part 4, p. 853.

2. Harry Cohen, *The Demonics of Bureaucracy* (Ames: Iowa State University Press, 1965), p. 142.

3. James Bovard, "Feeding Everybody: How Federal Food Programs Grew and Grew," *Policy Review* 26 (Fall 1983), pp. 43–44.

4. Martin Morse Wooster, "The Homeless Issue: An Adman's Dream," *Reason*, July 1987, pp. 20–28; the *Wall Street Journal*, September 3, 1987.

5. Ibid., p. 23.

6. *Rural Development, Agriculture, and Related Agencies Appropriations for 1988* (Hearings before a subcommittee of the Committee on Appropriations, House of Representatives, 100th Congress, 1st Session), part 5, p. 200.

7. The Food and Nutrition Service represented 0.01869 of the total federal budget in 1987. Assuming that it had a typical number of evaluation contracts, the

total spent on such contracts by the entire government can be projected at $1,874,719,000. An effort by the Comptroller General to tabulate all the federal evaluations conducted in 1984 came up with a total of 1,676. Assuming an average cost per evaluation of $900,000 (from Table 2.2), this figure indicates a federal expenditure of $1,508,400,000 on evaluations in that year. Comptroller General, *Federal Evaluations 1984* (1984 Congressional Sourcebook Series: GAO/AFMD-85-2), p. ix.

8. Resources and Technology Division, Economic Research Service, U.S. Department of Agriculture, *Ethanol: Economic and Policy Tradeoffs* (Agricultural Economic Report No. 585, April 1988), p. 42.

9. Sar A. Levitan and Gregory K. Wurzburg, *Evaluating Federal Programs: An Uncertain Art* (Kalamazoo, Mich.: W. E. Upjohn Institute for Employment Research, 1979), p. 123ff.

10. Richard F. Elmore, "Knowledge Development under the Youth Employment and Demonstration Projects Act, 1977–1981" in Charles L. Betsey, Robinson G. Hollister, Jr., and Mary R. Papageorgiou, eds., Youth Employment and Training Programs: The YEDPA Years (Washington, D.C.: National Academy Press, 1985), p. 341.

11. Betsey et al., *Youth Employment and Training Programs*, p. viii.

12. Ibid., p. 22.

13. Robert Moffit, "Symposium on the Econometric Evaluation of Manpower Training Programs: Introduction," *Journal of Human Resources* 22, no. 2 (Spring 1987), pp. 149–56; James Bovard, "The Failure of Federal Job Training," Cato Institute Policy Analysis No. 77 (August 28, 1986). The editors of the *New York Times* (April 15, 1987) have concluded that "the government has not been notably successful in job and skills training in the past." Alas, wholly wedded to the presumption of governmental efficacy, they continue, "but that's no reason to quit trying."

14. *Job Corps Oversight Hearing* (Hearing before the Subcommittee on Employment Opportunities of the Committee on Education and Labor, House of Representatives, 99th Congress, 2nd Session), pp. 21, 32–47, 53, 76.

15. Charles Mallar et al., *Evaluation of the Economic Impact of the Job Corps Program, Third Follow-Up Report* (Princeton, N.J.: Mathematica Policy Research, 1982), p. xiv.

16. Ibid., pp. 134, 136.

17. Ibid.

18. *Job Corps Oversight Hearing*, p. 21.

19. Mallar, pp. 133–36.

20. "The Budget's Hidden Horrors," *Time*, January 18, 1988, pp. 18–19.

21. *New York Times*, December 16, 1972.

22. Alan Parachini, "Sic Transit Transbus," *Reason*, July 1980, p. 34ff.

23. W. D. Dobson, "Will USDA Farm Programs Remain Highly Resistant to Change?" *American Journal of Agricultural Economics* 67, no. 2 (May 1985), pp. 331–35.

24. William Spangar Peirce, *Bureaucratic Failure and Public Expenditure* (New York: Academic Press, 1981).

25. *Congressional Record*, 98th Congress, 2nd Session (June 6, 1984), p. H5283.

26. Ibid., pp. H5283, H5284.

27. *Rural Development, Agriculture, and Related Agencies Appropriations for 1988*, part 5, p. 797.

28. *New York Times*, August 13, 1989.

29. Ibid.

30. John Calvin, *Institutes of the Christian Religion,* in Francis William Coker, ed., *Readings in Political Philosophy,* rev. ed. (New York: Macmillan, 1938), p. 337.

31. A. G. Dickens, *Reformation and Society in Sixteenth-Century Europe* (London: Harcourt, Brace, 1966), p. 164. Two of the best-known dissenters killed under Calvin were Jacques Gruet who was beheaded for blasphemy and Michael Servetus who was burned at the stake for his anti-Trinitarian views.

32. Calvin, p. 338.

Chapter 3

1. For a classic, well-written introduction to this issue, see Henry Hazlitt, *Economics in One Lesson* (New York: Harper, 1946), especially pp. 19–26.

2. Joseph A. Pechman, *Who Paid the Taxes, 1966–85?* (Washington, D.C.: Brookings Institution, 1985), pp. 60–62; Richard Goode, "The Income Tax: Effects on Distribution of Income and Wealth," in James G. Scoville, ed., *Perspectives on Poverty and Income Distribution* (Lexington, Mass.: D. C. Heath, 1971), pp. 167–77; Morgan Reynolds and Eugene Smolensky, *Public Expenditures, Taxes and the Distribution of Income* (New York: Academic Press, 1977). A comprehensive study of the incidence of taxation by the Tax Foundation finds that for federal taxes, the lowest income group (under $10,000) pays a greater proportion of its income in taxes than any other group except the over-$90,000 income group: *Tax Burden by Income Class, 1986–1987* (Washington, D.C.: Tax Foundation, 1989), p. 25.

3. Gordon Tullock, *Economics of Income Redistribution* (Boston: Kluwer-Nijhoff, 1983), p. 93ff.; Robert D. Reischauer, "The Federal Budget: Subsidies for the Rich," in Michael J. Boskin and Aaron Wildavsky, eds., *The Federal Budget: Economics and Politics* (San Francisco: Institute for Contemporary Studies, 1982), pp. 235–62; Peter J. Ferrara, "Intergenerational Transfers and Super IRA's," *The Cato Journal* 6, no. 1 (Spring/Summer 1986), pp. 195–220.

4. Clifton B. Luttrell, The High Cost of Farm Welfare (Washington: Cato Institute, 1989), pp. 113–30; E. C. Pasour, Jr., "The Farm Problem and Government Farm Programs," The Freeman, August 1987, pp. 303–7; Michael Fumento, "Some Dare Call Them Robber Barons," National Review, March 13, 1987, pp. 32–38. Typical of the nonredistributional character of farm programs were the "caps" placed on the payments in the 1988 drought relief bill. The maximum subsidy was set at $100,000, over five times the average taxpayer's wage, and payments were limited to those farmers whose gross income was less than $4,000,000; see Congressional Record, August 8, 1988, p. H6461. The actual income limit was $2,000,000, but when applied to those who make the majority of their income from farming, it grants the subsidy to a farmer whose total farm and nonfarm income is $4,000,000; see section 231 (b)(1).

5. Thomas J. DiLorenzo, "Why Government Jobs Programs Destroy Jobs," *The Freeman* 37, no. 11 (November 1987), pp. 428–30; Robert Jerrett, III, and Thomas A. Barocci, *Public Works, Government Spending, and Job Creation* (New York: Praeger, 1979), p. 1.

6. In 1985, 4,895,000 persons in households above the poverty level received food stamps; there were even 1,394,000 people in families with incomes over

$20,000 a year receiving food stamps. These figures understate the perverse income transfer involved, first, because true incomes are higher than those reported to Census Bureau pollsters and, second, because these income figures exclude the cash value of in-kind government benefits; U.S. Bureau of the Census, Current Population Reports, Series P-60, no. 155, *Receipt of Selected Noncash Benefits: 1985* (Washington, D.C.: Government Printing Office, 1987), pp. 24, 127.

7. *Job Corps: Its Costs, Employment Outcomes, and Service to the Public* (Washington, D.C.: General Accounting Office, July 1986), p. 8.

8. Howard M. Wachtel and Larry Sawyers, "Government Spending and the Distribution of Income," in Pamela Roby, ed., *The Poverty Establishment* (Englewood Cliffs, N.J.: Prentice-Hall, 1974), pp. 63–104. This pattern of nonredistributive spending is not confined to the United States. Surveying the evidence in Great Britain, one researcher concluded, "Almost all public expenditure on the social services in Britain benefits the better-off to a greater extent than the poor." See Julian Le Grand, *The Strategy of Equality: Redistribution and the Social Services* (London: George Allen & Unwin, 1982), p. 3.

9. On the taxation side, it appears that the collection system adds about 65 cents of costs for every dollar collected; see the Appendix, "Fallacies of Cost–Benefit Analysis." On the disbursement side, a number of separate costs trace both to the inefficiency of government operation and to economic distortions introduced by subsidies. The inefficiency cost alone appears to be 50 cents for each dollar spent. A comprehensive review of the cost of government services in fields as diverse as education, weather forecasting, and ambulance service sustained the "bureaucratic rule of two," that governmental production of the typical good or service costs twice as much as the same thing produced privately; James T. Bennett and Manuel H. Johnson, *Better Government at Half the Price: Private Production of Public Services* (Ottawa, Ill.: Caroline House, 1981), pp. 37–73.

10. *Congressional Record*, 98th Congress, 2nd Session (April 2, 1984), p. H 2133.

11. Congressional Quarterly, *Weekly Report*, October 24, 1987, p. 2584.

12. *Tributes to the Honorable Hugh Scott of Pennsylvania* (Senate Document 94–271, 94th Congress, 2nd Session), p. 3.

13. *Department of Housing and Urban Development—Independent Agencies Appropriations for 1988* (Hearings before a subcommittee of the Committee on Appropriations, House of Representatives, 100th Congress, 1st Session), part 8, pp. 230, 232.

Chapter 4

1. James D. Savage, *Balanced Budgets and American Politics* (Ithaca, N.Y.: Cornell University Press, 1988), pp. 91–97.

2. Richard F. Fenno, "The House Appropriations Committee as a Political System: The Problem of Integration," *American Political Science Review* 56 (June 1962), p. 311. The quotation is from the official committee history drawn up in 1941; Fenno found that in the 1950s committee members still shared the "guardian of the Treasury" outlook.

3. Aaron Wildavsky, *The Politics of the Budgetary Process*, 3d ed. (Boston: Little, Brown, 1979), p. 35ff.

4. Harvey C. Mansfield, Sr., "General Accounting Office," in Donald R. Whitnah, ed., *Government Agencies* (Westport, Conn.: Greenwood Press, 1983), p. 266.

5. *USDA's Commodity Program: The Accuracy of Budget Forecasts* (Washington, D.C.: General Accounting Office, April 1988), p. 74.

6. From the data given in ibid., p. 36, predicting each year's expenditures from the previous year's will produce a mean absolute error of $4.1 billion, compared to $4.3 billion for Department of Agriculture estimates. The mean net error would be $1.55 billion, half the Department's error of $3.1 billion.

7. Ibid., p. 73.

8. *Washington Post*, April 18, 1988.

9. *Rural Development, Agriculture, and Related Agencies Appropriations for 1988* (Hearings), part 6, pp. 213–14.

10. Full details about this episode came to light when Congressman Henry B. Gonzalez contested the CBS footage and the hospital examined its records; *Congressional Record*, July 31, 1968, pp. 24432–35; September 12, 1968, pp. 26625–26.

11. James Bovard, "Feeding Everybody: How Federal Food Programs Grew and Grew," *Policy Review* 26 (Fall 1983), pp. 43–44.

12. The producer of "Hunger in America," Martin Carr, explained his strategy of making "documentaries" in a talk he gave in 1978. His approach is to take his own "point of view" on the topic and then "make a film that is going to make you feel the way I feel about it." Accuracy in Media, *AIM Report*, October 1979, supplement, p. 1.

13. *Washington Post*, April 18, 1988.

14. One of the components of media distortion on spending issues is the use of the "current services budget." These are estimates produced by administration budgetmakers, stating budgetary "needs," taking into account inflation, congressional expansion of services, and demographic changes. In principle, these estimates show what level of spending is needed to keep program benefits at their current real levels. Aside from exaggerating even these needs, the current services estimates have led to a shocking debasement of language whereby budget increases are reported and discussed as "cuts." For example, from 1980 to 1989, medicare spending has gone from $32 billion to over $80 billion. Since the current services projections report a budget "need" of $129 billion in 1989, the 1989 spending can be said to represent a "cut" of $49 billion. Journalists advocating spending programs use these misleading "current services" figures to give official status to their claims that programs have been "cut" when, in fact, spending on them has increased.

15. *TV News Covers the Budget Debate* (Washington, D.C.: The Media Institute, 1986), p. 19. The breakdown was 277 lines favorable to COLA spending, 99 lines unfavorable, and 38 lines classified as neutral.

16. S. Robert Lichter, Stanley Rothman, and Linda S. Lichter, *The Media Elite* (Bethesda, Md.: Adler and Adler, 1986), pp. 28–43.

17. Ibid., p. 42.

18. James W. Chesebro, "Communication, Values, and Popular Television Series—An Eleven-Year Assessment," in Gary Gumpert and Robert Cathcart, eds., *Inter/media: Interpersonal Communication in a Media World* (New York: Oxford, 1966), p. 483ff.

19. Eric P. Veblen, "Liberalism and National Newspaper Coverage of Members of Congress," *Polity* 14 (Fall 1981), pp. 153–59.

Chapter 5

1. The Pearson product-moment correlation between the 1986 NTU ratings and the spending score developed in this study is –0.92 (NTU scores are "non-spending" scores and hence run in the opposite direction to my spending scores).

2. For 1984, I compiled a House spending score based on twelve votes, three each in the fields of agriculture, antipoverty spending, science/culture spending, and pro-business spending. For a listing of these votes, see "The True Spending Culprits," the *Wall Street Journal,* April 16, 1986. This produced a spending score with a maximum value of 12. Cross-tabulated with seniority, the results are as follows:

	Average Spending Score		
Seniority	Both parties	Democrats	Republicans
0 to 4 years (N = 140)	6.0	8.6	2.8
5 to 19 years (N = 231)	6.9	9.0	3.7
Over 20 years (N = 35)	8.7	9.9	4.7

3. A simple measure of the apprenticeship effect for the data given in Figure 5.1 is to subtract the second-year score from the first-year score. (If there were no apprenticeship effect at all, this operation would yield a negative value.) Subdivided by party, these are the results:

	First-year score	Second-year score	Apprenticeship effect
With prior government office			
Democrats (N = 37)	–1.51	–2.76	1.25
Republicans (N = 9)	–3.44	–4.11	0.67
Without prior government office			
Democrats (N = 9)	–7.22	–12.78	5.56
Republicans (N = 4)	–6.75	–7.50	0.75

We see from this tabulation that House Democrats exhibit a greater apprenticeship effect than do Republicans. That is, in their first year in Congress, Democrats deviate more sharply from their own (lower-spending) preferences in conforming to the big-spending party leadership.

4. For example, on a House energy and water appropriations bill in 1986 (HR 5162, CQ vote number 221), Representative Bill Frenzel (R–Minn.) proposed an amendment to reduce spending, a reduction publicly opposed by Reagan. Nevertheless, it was the Democrats who sided with President Reagan to oppose the amendment and preserve the higher spending figure; 78 percent of the Democrats voted for the higher spending and only 33 percent of the Republicans did. This

45-point spread between the parties is typical of the party break on spending, and therefore indicates little tendency of Republicans to follow President Reagan's leadership when that leadership was exerted in a prospending direction.

5. Martin Tolchin, "The Perplexing Mr. Proxmire," *The New York Times Magazine*, May 28, 1978, p. 56.

6. William Proxmire, *Uncle Sam—Last of the Bigtime Spenders* (New York: Simon and Schuster, 1972), pp. 9–12.

Chapter 6

1. See the discussion of this point in Chapter 3.

2. For a critique of EDA and UDAG see Fred Barnes, "Who's to Blame for the Deficit," *Reader's Digest*, May 1986, pp. 112–116. Barnes declared (p. 116) that UDAG money "goes for commercial development, not aid to the poor. Wealthy hotel chains—such as Hilton, Hyatt and Holiday Inn—received dozens of grants." Concerning the Small Business Administration, another press report declared that, "For all its loan programs, consulting services and grants, it is doubtful the Small Business Administration has made much difference, one way or the other, in the basic nature or extent of small business in the United States." Tom Teepen, "GOP Looking Out for Its Clients or the SBA Would Be History" (Cox News Service), *The Spokesman-Review* (Spokane), September 8, 1986.

3. Fred Barnes, "Through the Looking Glass: Washington, D.C.," *Imprimis* 15, no. 7 (July 1986), p. 5.

4. In the House, 81 percent of the Democrats voted for the Chrysler bailout as opposed to 41 percent of the Republicans. In the Senate, 71 percent of the Democrats supported it, as opposed to 31 percent of the Republicans.

5. See, for example, Barnes, "Who's to Blame for the Deficit," Teepen, "GOP Looking Out for Its Clients," and Joann S. Lublin, "An Agency Even the President Can't Scuttle," the *Wall Street Journal*, August 18, 1986. This last piece incorrectly asserted that the congressional supporters of SBA were "largely Republican." Compare this allegation to the facts: On the July 17, 1986 House vote to discontinue the ordinary SBA loan program, 94 percent of the Democrats voted to continue the loan program, as opposed to only 31 percent of the Republicans. For the background of this error and an explanation of why it continues to be made, see James L. Payne, "Fatcats and Democrats," *National Review*, November 21, 1986, p. 34, and James L. Payne, "The True Spending Culprits," the *Wall Street Journal*, April 16, 1986.

6. In the 1986 rating, the ADA used the vote for the Omnibus Trade Bill, which contained a number of trade "retaliation" provisions, as a positive vote. *ADA Today* 42, no. 1 (January 1987), p. 7.

Chapter 7

1. *Wall Street Journal*, November 15, 1985.

2. Morris P. Fiorina, *Congress: Keystone of the Washington Establishment* (New Haven: Yale University Press, 1977), p. 73.

3. David A. Stockman, *The Triumph of Politics: The Inside Story of the Reagan Revolution* (New York: Avon Books, 1987), p. 409.

4. I refer to the employer-contributed social security tax, which matches that contributed by the worker. This employer contribution is really a further tax against the worker's wages. To visualize this connection, imagine Congress passes a law that says all employer contributions shall be given to the worker in his paycheck, and the worker shall be taxed an additional amount exactly equal to the former employer contributions. Under this rearrangement, net taxes, wages, and employer labor costs would be identical, only the full tax burden on the employee would be visible.

5. Anthony Downs, An Economic Theory of Democracy (New York: Harper, 1957).

6. Downs, "Why the Government Budget Is Too Small in a Democracy," *World Politics* 12, no. 4 (July 1960), pp. 541–63.

7. Some of the findings from the 1982 University of Michigan post-election survey give a feel for the level of voter awareness: Only 34 percent could recall the name of even one congressional candidate; only 37 percent of the sample could identify Ronald Reagan as conservative (this figure has been corrected for guessing); only 3 percent of the sample knew that the House of Representatives was controlled by the Democrats (figure corrected for guessing). See Warren E. Miller, *American National Election Study, 1982: Post-Election Survey File* (Ann Arbor: Inter-University Consortium for Political and Social Research, 1983), pp. 73, 220, 290.

In a 1984 survey concerning defense spending, only 6 percent of the respondents said, correctly, that defense spending was less than 10 percent of the GNP. A clear majority, 57 percent, said that defense spending was 20 percent of GNP (three times as high as the actual figure), and 9 percent said it exceeded 50 percent of GNP. See Committee on the Present Danger, *Defense and the Deficit* (Washington, D.C.: 1985), p. 4.

A comprehensive effort to measure citizen awareness of the positions of U.S. Representatives came up with the findings that fewer than half of the survey respondents were even willing to guess where their representative stood on major issues, and that on any given issue, no more than 5 percent could be said to know the representative's position (this figure includes a correction for guessing). On the one spending issue included in the survey, spending for the Legal Services Corporation—a major, controversial issue at the time of the survey (1978)—only 16 respondents out of 2,023 (0.7 percent) knew their representative's position (corrected for guessing). The study also revealed that the public's ability to identify the issue positions of candidates was vastly lower when it came to challengers. For the rational voting theory to work, of course, the voter must know the position of both candidates. This study strongly suggests that for the typical spending measure, there may not be even *one* voter who knows the position of both the incumbent and his challenger in the typical House election. See Patricia A. Hurley and Kim Quaile Hill, "The Prospects for Issue-Voting in Contemporary Congressional Elections: An Assessment of Citizen Awareness and Representation," *American Politics Quarterly* 8, no. 4 (October 1980), pp. 425–48.

8. For a comprehensive survey of the evidence showing that congressmen's policy positions are not controlled by constituents through the electoral process, see

Robert A. Bernstein, *Elections, Representation, and Congressional Voting Behavior: The Myth of Constituency Control* (Englewood Cliffs, N.J.: Prentice-Hall, 1989).

9. Donald E. Stokes and Warren E. Miller, "Party Government and the Saliency of Congress," in Angus Campbell et al., *Elections and the Political Order* (New York: Wiley, 1966), chap. 11.

10. Thomas E. Mann, *Unsafe at Any Margin: Interpreting Congressional Elections* (Washington, D.C.: American Enterprise Institute, 1978), chaps. 2 and 3; Barbara Hinckley, *Congressional Elections* (Washington, D.C.: Congressional Quarterly Press, 1981), chaps. 2–6.

11. J. Peter Grace, *Burning Money: The Waste of Your Tax Dollars* (New York: Macmillan, 1984), p. 8.

12. Paul Feldman and James Jondrow, "Congressional Elections and Local Federal Spending," American Journal of Political Science 28, no. 1 (February 1984), p. 155.

13. *Congressional Record*, June 6, 1983, pp. H3638–51.

14. *Congressional Record*, June 21, 1984, pp. H6286–90.

15. *Congressional Record*, August 7, 1986, pp. H5652–63.

16. *Congressional Record*, September 8, 1975, pp. 27816–17; *Milwaukee Journal*, January 11, 1976; *La Crosse Tribune*, January 11, 1976.

17. Averaging the 1964 and 1970 election results, Proxmire ran 6.9 percentage points lower in Vernon County than statewide. After his action on the Kickapoo Dam, his electoral strength in 1976 and 1982 averaged 16.4 percentage points below his statewide strength. Hence, the electoral effect attributable to the Kickapoo controversy can be estimated as –9.5 percentage points (–16.4 – [–6.9]).

18. Congressional Quarterly, *Weekly Report*, October 24, 1987, p. 2584.

19. Ibid.

20. Ibid., p. 2592.

21. Louis Anthony Dexter, "The Representative and His District," in Robert L. Peabody and Nelson W. Polsby, eds., *New Perspectives on the House of Representatives* (Chicago: Rand McNally, 1963), pp. 3–29.

22. Congressional Quarterly, *Weekly Report*, October 24, 1987, p. 2592.

23. In 1984, there were nine retirees—seven Republicans and two Democrats. Using the twelve-issue spending score described in Note 2, Chapter 5, the respective scores are as follows:

| | 1984 Spending Score (Max. = 12) | |
	Democrats	Republicans
Retirees	9.8 (N = 2)	3.4 (N = 7)
Nonretirees	9.0 (N = 240)	3.4 (N = 157)

24. John R. Hibbing, "The Liberal Hour: Electoral Pressures and Transfer Payment Voting in the United States Congress," The Journal of Politics 46 (1984), pp. 846–65.

25. Congressional Quarterly, *Weekly Report*, October 24, 1987, p. 2592.

26. Albert D. Cover and Bruce S. Brumberg, "Baby Books and Ballots: The Impact of Congressional Mail on Constituent Opinion," *American Political Science Review* 76, no. 2 (June 1982), pp. 347–59.

27. When vote change is regressed on party and 1986 spending scores, the following multiple regression equation results:

Variable	Coefficient	Standard error	T-score
Party	–6.91	1.75	–3.95
Spending score	–0.06	0.07	–0.75
Constant	15.70	3.96	3.97
$R^2 = .15; N = 196$			

The dependent variable, vote change, is calculated by subtracting the congressman's percentage in the 1984 election from his percentage in the 1986 election; party is entered as a dichotomous variable, 1 = Democrat, 2 = Republican; the spending score is the congressman's spending score based on thirty-six domestic spending votes, as described in the Appendix, "Measuring Congressional Spending." The regression is based on the 196 cases defined in Table 7.3, note a.

The coefficient for the spending score of –0.06 implies that voting for domestic spending *hurts* a congressman's electoral margin, rather than helping it as the electoral theory predicts. This trend is too weak to be statistically significant, however. The best overall conclusion is that voting for spending has no effect on a congressman's electoral margin.

28. The multiple regression equation has the following values (the dependent variable is the congressman's 1986 spending score, described in the Appendix, "Measuring Congressional Spending"):

Variable	Coefficient	Standard error	T-score
Party	–19.3	0.665	–29.05
Seniority	0.378	0.087	4.32
Vote 1984 (lim.)	–0.03	0.04	–0.74
Constant	48.93	2.72	17.98
$R^2 = 0.70; N = 414$			

The party variable is 1 for Democrats, 2 for Republicans; seniority is entered as terms served; "vote 1984 (lim.)" is the percentage of the two-party vote the congressman received in the 1984 election, with values over 75 converted to 75—under the assumption that values over 75 do not reflect greater degrees of electoral security. The coefficient for this variable has the correct sign, but is statistically insignificant. Another way to assess its importance is to compare the vote effect with the effect of party and seniority when all values are allowed to shift across their entire real range (from 1 to 2 for party, from 1 to 23 for seniority, and from 49 to 75 for vote 1984). Using this technique, the effect of party turns out to be 24.9 times as important as vote 1984 on the congressman's spending score; the effect of seniority is 10.7 times as important.

29. Charles Peters, *How Washington Really Works* (Reading, Mass.: Addison-Wesley, 1980), p. 7.

Chapter 8

1. Office of Management and Budget, *Historical Tables: Budget of the United States Government, Fiscal Year 1989* (Washington, D.C.: Government Printing Office, 1988), Table 6.1.

2. Tax Foundation, *Facts and Figures on Government Finance* (Washington, D.C.: 1986), Table a33; James L. Payne, "Marxism and Militarism," *Polity* 19, no. 2 (Winter 1986), pp. 270–89, especially table 4; Payne, *Why Nations Arm* (Oxford: Basil Blackwell, 1989), chap. 14.

3. The simple regression of the thirty-six-vote nonmilitary spending score against the five-vote military spending score as the dependent variable produces an R^2 of 0.47. When the variable of party is added as an independent variable, the resulting multiple regression equation has an R^2 of 0.50. I interpret this to mean that party adds only .03 to the explained variance, and therefore could be said to have only a small independent effect in determining a congressman's position on military spending.

4. Herbert McClosky, Paul J. Hoffman, and Rosemary O'Hara, "Issue Conflict and Consensus among Party Leaders and Followers," *American Political Science Review* 54 (June 1960), p. 415; Julius Turner, *Party and Constituency: Pressures on Congress*, revised by Edward V. Schneier, Jr. (Baltimore: Johns Hopkins Press, 1970), pp. 68–70.

5. Office of the Assistant Secretary of Defense (Comptroller), *National Defense Budget Estimates for FY 1987* (Washington, D.C.: Government Printing Office, 1986), Table 7–6.

6. See remarks in the *Congressional Record*, June 15, 1984, pp. H5931–32.

7. An unstated assumption of this analysis is that one is dealing with an antimilitary culture—which is the case for the United States (see text below). In a militaristic culture, the manifest aspect of weapons and war, even in peacetime, could be appealing.

In *Why Nations Arm* (chap. 11), I explain how this changeable orientation toward military forces and war underlies Anglo-American military behavior. One dramatic example of this changeable attitude toward the use of force was Sen. George McGovern, who was a leading opponent of American involvement in Vietnam, but who called for military reinvolvement in Southeast Asia once communist atrocities there dominated the news; see Payne, "Foreign Policy for an Impulsive People" in Aaron Wildavsky, ed., *Beyond Containment* (San Francisco: Institute for Contemporary Studies, 1983), pp. 215–16. Another N-liberal whose opposition to the use of force is erratic is Sen. Howard Metzenbaum. Normally, the senator is a foe of defense and intelligence activities, yet during the hysteria about Libya's involvement in terrorism against U.S. citizens, Metzenbaum advocated assassination of Libyan leader Muammar Qaddafi; see the *New York Times*, January 10, 1986.

8. *Why Nations Arm*, chaps. 11 and 13.

9. The concept of "military effort" expresses defense spending in relation to a nation's discretionary resources. For an explanation of this concept and its measurement, see *Why Nations Arm*, chaps. 2, 3, and 14.

10. *The Gallup Report*, May 1987, p. 3; *The Gallup Report*, March 1985, p. 4.

11. In a 1984 poll, only 6 percent of the respondents said, correctly, that defense spending was less than 10 percent of the GNP; Committee on the Present Danger, *Defense and the Deficit* (Washington, D.C.: 1985), p. 4. In a 1969 Gallup poll, respondents

were asked to state the fraction of federal spending that went to defense. The results were that 71 percent were unable to answer, 15 percent guessed far too high, 6 percent guessed far too low, and only 8 percent were close enough to be considered correct. In addition to documenting the U.S. public's tendency to overestimate defense spending, this survey illustrates how poorly informed voters are about the budget. The 8 percent who were "correct" are easily explained by lucky guessing; perhaps virtually no one actually knew the correct answer. George H. Gallup, *The Gallup Poll; Public Opinion 1935–1971*, vol. 3 (New York: Random House, 1972), p. 2210.

12. *Mid Atlantic January 1987 Grassroots Peace Directory* (Pomfret, Conn.: Topsfield Foundation, 1986).

13. Resource Center for Nonviolence, *Disarmament Directory* (Santa Cruz, Calif.: 1984).

14. Institute for Defense and Disarmament Studies, *Peace Resource Book* (Cambridge, Mass.: Ballinger, 1986).

15. The 1985 Media Institute study of forty-six television stories on defense spending found that antispending material outweighed prospending issues by over two to one (65.5 percent to 31.1 percent), *TV News Covers the Budget Debate* (Washington, D.C.: The Media Institute, 1986), p. 34. See also *Why Nations Arm*, chap. 13.

16. Ideally, one would like a longitudinal analysis to confirm this point, as was done in Chapter 5 to confirm the seniority effect. It is possible that the promilitary attitude of committee members existed before they joined the committee: It could have been the reason why they joined, or were selected to join.

Chapter 9

1. James L. Payne, *Patterns of Conflict in Colombia* (New Haven: Yale, 1968), p. 268ff.

2. For a survey of how federal and state governments get around many existing spending limitations, see James Bennett and Thomas DiLorenzo, *Underground Government* (Washington, D.C.: Cato Institute, 1983).

3. *Weekly Compilation of Presidential Documents*, vol. 10 (July 15, 1974), p. 800.

4. John W. Ellwood, "The Great Exception: The Congressional Budget Process in an Age of Decentralization," in Lawrence C. Dodd and Bruce I. Oppenheimer, *Congress Reconsidered*, 3rd ed. (Washington, D.C.: CQ Press, 1985), pp. 315–42.

5. *Congressional Quarterly Weekly Report*, vol. 43, no. 50 (December 14, 1985), p. 2604.

6. General Accounting Office, *Deficit Reductions for Fiscal Year 1990; Compliance with the Balanced Budget and Emergency Deficit Control Act of 1985* (Washington, D.C.: November 1989), p. 5.

7. Scott A. Hodge, "Budget 'Savings' Mean More Taxes," the *Wall Street Journal*, November 9, 1990.

8. David Rogers, "Changes Overseas Reshaped 1991 Spending Legislation," the *Wall Street Journal*, October 29, 1990; Jeffrey H. Birnbaum, "Wrenching Battle on Deficit Reduction Points to More Contests in Years Ahead," ibid.

9. David A. Stockman, *The Triumph of Politics* (New York: Avon Books, 1987), p. 122.

10. Office of Management and Budget, *Budget of the U.S. Government, Fiscal Year 1989* (Washington, D.C.: Government Printing Office, 1988), pp. 5–56.

11. *New York Times*, June 14, 1988. In 1987, the Reagan administration was so stung by accusations about having cut programs that it produced a special document to rebut such charges: *The FY 1988 Budget: Assertions vs. Facts*, Office of Management and Budget, February 1987. Although the document made a few references to the administration's efforts to apply free-market principles to the economy, its main point was that charges that the administration had cut programs were false, since it had increased them. For example, on veterans' programs (p. 26), the "assertion" was that "there are big cuts in veterans' health care"; the "fact" set forth to rebut this was that "outlays for veterans' hospitals and medical care will rise to a record level of $10.5 billion in 1988, from $10.3 billion in 1987."

12. *Time*, November 7, 1988, p. 7.

13. *Time*, November 14, 1988, p. 7.

Chapter 10

1. Statement of Richard A. Snelling, Chairman, Proposition One, Inc., in *Department of Housing and Urban Development, and Certain Independent Agencies Appropriations for Fiscal Year 1986* (Hearings before a subcommittee of the Committee on Appropriations, Senate, 99th Congress, 1st Session), part 3, p. 2047ff.

2. *Rural Development, Agriculture, and Related Agencies Appropriations for 1990* (Hearings before a subcommittee of the Committee on Appropriations, House of Representatives, 101st Congress, 1st Session), part 7, p. 443.

3. Ibid., p. 444.

Chapter 11

1. Of the twenty-four junior-senior comparisons (twelve in the Democratic party and twelve in the Republican party), the juniors were more fiscally conservative in twenty-three. In the 1989 ratings for Democrats, junior and senior Democrats have the same average NTU rating.

2. Of the twenty-four comparisons, the junior senators were more fiscally conservative than the seniors in their own party in seventeen cases. It should be noted that the junior-senior effect seen in Tables 11.1 and 11.2 reflects both an indoctrination effect and a composition effect. The senior contingent in both House and Senate has a higher proportion of Democrats than the junior contingent. The reason for this composition imbalance is that Republicans have a higher rate of voluntary retirement.

3. *Wall Street Journal*, October 29, 1990; Scott A. Hodge, "Budget 'Savings' Mean More Taxes," the *Wall Street Journal*, November 9, 1990. All figures refer to five-year totals.

4. Albert R. Hunt (head of the Washington Bureau of *The Wall Street Journal*), "Congress's Terms: Just Fine as They Are," the *Wall Street Journal*, April 24, 1990.

5. Thomas Mann, political scientist at the Brookings Institution, quoted in ibid.

6. Rudy Boschwitz, Republican Senator from Minnesota, quoted in David Shribman, "Drive to Restrict Tenure in Congress to Twelve Years Is Pressed in Capital and One-Third of the States," the *Wall Street Journal,* March 12, 1990.

Appendix

1. This figure is the author's summation from his forthcoming *Hosting the Federal Banquet.* One of the main findings supporting this calculation comes from the Arthur D. Little survey of the federal tax compliance burden on both businesses and individuals, *Development of Methodology for Estimating the Taxpayer Paperwork Burden* (Washington, D.C.: Internal Revenue Service, 1988). This study found that the 1985 compliance burden was more than five billion hours. When priced at the market cost for tax workers, the value of this labor comes to 24 percent of available tax revenues collected.

One comprehensive calculation of the disincentive or "deadweight" economic loss attributable to the tax system has been put forward by Charles L. Ballard, John B. Shoven, and John Whalley, "General Equilibrium Computations of the Marginal Welfare Costs of Taxes in the United States" in *The American Economic Review* (March 1985), pp. 128–138. They found that the marginal excess burden per additional tax dollar ranged from 17 to 56 cents, depending on the assumptions supplied for elasticities of labor and savings. Using middle values for each variable, their calculations indicate a loss of 33 cents per tax dollar collected.

Hence these two studies alone indicate an overhead cost of 57 cents per tax dollar collected.

Index